D0180281

How To Be Wanted:
Use the Law of Attraction to Date the Man You Most Desire and Live the Life You Deserve

Also by Romy Miller:

Understanding Women: The Definitive Guide to Meeting, Dating and Dumping, if Necessary

Man Magnet: How to be the Best Woman So You Can Get the Best Man

How To Be Wanted:
Use the Law of Attraction to Date the Man You Most Desire and Live the Life You Deserve

By

Romy Miller

The Book Factory

How To Be Wanted: Use the Law of Attraction to Date the Man
You Most Desire and Live the Life You Deserve
by
Romy Miller

The Book Factory
an imprint of New Tradition Books
ISBN 1932420770

For information contact:
The Book Factory
newtraditionbooks@yahoo.com

"Life isn't about finding yourself. Life is about creating yourself."
George Bernard Shaw

For L.P.
You are the Law of Attraction in action.

Contents

Be safe.

I want to briefly touch on a subject that's quite important and that is safety. *You have to keep yourself safe.* I think it's obligatory to include a warning about some of the men you might run across. And I don't mean for this to be a downer, but we have to be safe in these days and times. We're women and we know there are a lot of creeps out there, unfortunately, and some of them want to hurt women. So, this goes without saying, but I will say it anyway: Be safe. Be aware. Be cautious. Always tell someone where you are going and with whom. Always listen to your gut, as it will let you know if something is askew with certain men.

Got it? Good. Let's get to the fun stuff.

It's raining men and you're about to get soaked.

In dating it's all about being wanted. But you can't always get what you want, right? Well, the Law of Attraction begs to differ.

In fact, I would venture to say that in life, it's all about being wanted as well. *Do they want me for the new job? Does the waitress want my tip badly enough to give me good service? Do the men I like want to take the chance to get to know me?* And the list goes on and on.

So if life is all about being wanted, how do you do this? You use the Law of Attraction to get it. Easy, right?

"Wait a minute," you protest, *"You want me to use the Law of Attraction to get the man of my dreams? Isn't that some kind of hokey, mumbo jumbo, metaphysical thing that hippies use when they're taking psychedelic drugs? Or is this the thing that they talk about in infomercials?"*

Uh, no, not exactly.

Haven't you always wanted to be "that girl"? I bet you have. You know the girl I'm talking about. She's pretty and cute and she gets just about everything she wants out of life—from the best jobs to the best clothes to the best men. She knows that it's raining men and she's getting soaked.

That girl can be you.

You *can* have any man you want. You *can* have the life you deserve. And all you have to do is take the first step. And the first step is nothing more than knowing what you want. And beyond that? Well, that's what this book is all about. It's about how to attract the man and life of your dreams by not only utilizing the Law of Attraction but also your God-given female assets. By the time we're through, you will have everything you need to go out and get that man—or men—and also the life you deserve.

Sprinkled throughout the book are chapters on how to be wanted, things you can do to make it happen, along with advice about why you should do it and how. The other chapters discuss things that might be blocking you from getting what you want out of life, consequently blocking your full potential.

A lot of the book, however, is concentrated on the Law of Attraction. You might sometimes wonder, "What does all this have to do with getting a man?" And to that I say, "Everything!" Until you begin attracting good things into your life through the Law of Attraction, a good man can't be attracted, either.

Also, please note that this is *my* take on the Law of Attraction. You might have read other books on this subject and wonder why mine isn't identical to those. Well, this is my interpretation and how I've applied it to my life and, when asked, told others how to use it as well. This isn't your cookie-cutter Law of Attraction or dating book. What I want this one to give you is a real, hands-on approach to how it works, why it works and how you can make it work for you, by both landing a good man and getting the life you deserve.

The point of this book is to get you ready to go out there and get the man and the life you want and desire. This process of manifesting desires will bring you to that point of embracing what you truly want out of life.

So, yeah, it is raining men and you are about to get soaked. By the way, leave your umbrella at home.

Like attracts like.

Many people don't understand, or even realize, what the Law of Attraction is. The odd thing is, it's really no secret and it's not that hard to comprehend. Anyone in any walk of life can do it. I can do it. You can do it, too. So what is it? Metaphysical mumbo-jumbo? Something a yoga guru teaches his followers? No, not exactly.

The Law of Attraction is this: Like attracts like. Whatever is in your life now, you have attracted. But you protest, *"No! I haven't done this. This bad dating stretch or all the horrible men or the unsavory unhappiness is just because of extenuating circumstances. I didn't cause it. Not me! I haven't done this to myself."*

Methinks you doth protest too much. Stop for a minute and think about it. Now think about the Law of Attraction—like attracts like.

Like attracts like. What *does* that mean? Simply put, whatever vibe you're putting out will come back to you. Say you want a vanilla ice cream cone. You haven't had one for years but all of a sudden, you want one and you want it bad. Does the vanilla ice cream cone just come to you? No, you have to go out and get it. This is taking action. So, in theory, if you *like* a vanilla ice cream cone, you will *get* a vanilla ice cream cone because the vanilla ice cream cone likes you, too. All you have to do is make yourself available to *receive* the vanilla ice cream cone and you can do that easy. There are lots of places to get ice cream. Because you know what you want—a vanilla ice cream cone—you're going to put yourself in a position where you're going to get a vanilla ice cream cone. This happens on both a conscious and subconscious level.

And, yes, this applies to your dating style as well.

Say, for instance, you *think* you like a certain kind of man. He may be a bad boy or a loser or whatever. However, he's all wrong for you. But, deep down, you don't *really* like this kind of man; you just think this is the kind of man you will inevitably end up with. And so you do. And why do you always end up with this loser? Because you've lowered your expectations and, by doing that, you're attracting a lower class of guy.

It's about your expectations. Even more simply put, it's about a sense of entitlement.

Most of us don't grow up with silver spoons and, therefore, we don't feel like we're exactly entitled to too much from this world. So, we settle. We settle for a lesser job, a lesser house, a lesser man and, pretty much, a lesser life. As we settle for this and for that, we are attracting what we think we deserve out of life—less. And that's what we get. Like attracts like.

However, say you grew up in a wealthy family. Maybe you were so rich you had a bowling alley in your house. Maybe you had servants and didn't have to pick up after yourself. Maybe your parents bought you the perfect car for your sixteenth birthday and gave you the keys as you were cutting your fabulous chocolate truffle birthday cake. This gives you a sense of entitlement. So, as you go through life, you're going to keep that sense of entitlement. You won't date a man who can't afford your affluent lifestyle. You won't wear clothes that aren't from certain stores and you certainly won't vacation in the wrong places. You will expect more out of life and you will get it. Like attracts like.

Its sounds so wrong, doesn't it? It sounds like it wouldn't work quite like that. You may be thinking about the rich girl I just described in the last paragraph. You may be feeling a little resentment. *Why does she get all this and I don't get anything? One day, she'll get hers, alright, and she'll get it* bad, *and she won't like it.*

If your thoughts are along these lines, you are so missing the point.

Besides, some bad things might happen to her because sometimes bad things happen in life. However, this has nothing to do with the fact that she will inevitably lead a much better life than someone with low expectations. However, it doesn't matter what the rich girl does. In fact, it *shouldn't* matter. If it does matter to you, you are not putting out a positive vibe, i.e. a positive attitude, and, therefore, you are going to get more of what you put out back: Deficiency. To resent others for what they have is coming from a place of lack. We think: *If she has it, that means I can't.*

No, no, no.

And this is my point. This is what this book is about. In order to be wanted and in order to date the man you most desire and, lastly, in order to get the life you deserve, you will have to completely and totally turn your head around. And I'm not talking about an *Exorcist* kind of way, either.

Throughout this book, I will be discussing how the Law of Attraction is at play in your life right now, whether you recognize it or not. I will tell you why you're not dating the man you want and what you can do about that. But, most importantly, I will tell you how you can overcome all this backward thinking we've all been ingrained with. And, yes, you're not the only one who has missed out on this wonderful thing called the Law of Attraction.

By the end of this book, I want you to be empowered. I want you to know beyond a shadow of a doubt that you can have the man you most desire. I want you to know you can have the life you deserve. By the end of this book, I want you to *feel* it because once you *feel* it, you'll have it.

The great thing is, whatever you have attracted doesn't matter because you can start today to attract better men and better situations. And by starting to use the Law of Attraction and getting a better attitude, along with higher expectations, you can have what you want. And what you mostly want is to be wanted because being wanted puts you in a position of power and receiving. And that's pretty good stuff.

Again— like attracts like.

The Law of Attraction simply states that like attracts like. Whatever you put out there will come back to you. And, no, we're not talking about Karma, either. This is not "what goes around comes around". This is about feeling in control of your life, right now. It's not about waiting for the ax to fall.

But how does it work? The Law of Attraction works through intention. Once you know what you want, you put out that intention: "I want_____." (Please feel free to fill in the blank.) Once the intention is out, sit back and wait. And is that all? Well, no. What is most important is to recognize your wants and truly *want* them. You have to want them so bad you can *feel* them coming to life through your imagination. If you do this, you will somehow get what you want. It may come in the form of an idea that occurs to you. It may be that you might begin to look at something in a different way and understand how you can get it. Conversely, the "how" is unimportant. It's the *desire* and the *recognition* of the desire that's important.

However, while you're waiting, don't think about it, don't obsess about how it's going to happen, release it and wait for the inspiration. (This is called letting go of the outcome.) The inspiration is what will come to your mind about what to do about your want, through ideas. Once this happens, take action.

In effect, you state your intention as though it has already manifested. "I am dating a good man!" Or even, "I will date a good man!" (You can use this for anything, as in "I will buy a designer purse!")

Do you get it? Here it is again, in five easy steps.

Five easy steps:
- Know what you want.
- Say what you want, i.e., put out your intention. "I want_____."
- Release. (Let go of the outcome.)
- Wait for inspiration and let the ideas begin to pop up in your head.
- Take action.

And is that all you have to do to get what you want? Yup. Don't believe me? Then read on. We've got a lot of work to do.

You have to know what you want.

You have to know what you want. In order to be wanted, you must first define what you want in a man, in a relationship and, most importantly, out of life.

One thing that might be keeping you from getting what you want out of life is the very fact that you don't know what you want. This seems, on the surface, an easy thing to do. Everyone knows what they want, right? Not so much. If you're uncertain about what it is that you want, whether it's a boyfriend or a new car, then none of it will ever come to you. And, even if it does, you'll never know when you actually get it. This is why it's so important to define what you want before doing anything else.

Knowing what you want is the exact opposite of knowing what you don't want. Once you figure out what you don't want, it's time to figure out what you do want. Keep in mind that if you have no idea of what you want, you'll inevitably end up in a less than ideal situation. But you don't have to! All you need to do to remedy this is to know what you want. By knowing what you want, you can always find a way to get it.

So, what, exactly, do you want? Define it. Sit down and write it out. Marriage? A white picket fence? An expensive penthouse in the city? Kids? It is imperative that you define whatever it is what you want so you can dream it, so you can begin to live it. Knowing what you want is so necessary to the Law of Attraction because if you know what you want, you can actually get it. Let me reiterate: Until you figure out exactly what you want, you'll never get it mainly because you won't ever know when you've gotten it because you don't know what it is. So, sit down and write it all out, therefore, defining what you want. This may take weeks and that's okay. Allow time for your desires to surface.

Once you know what you want, just state your desires. Remember: "I want_____." This will eventually lead to "I will_____." And once you start that, you are well on your way to better things in life.

This process isn't difficult, so don't make it difficult. Also, it should be fun! It's like going onto your favorite website on the internet and browsing for whatever you want and actually being able to afford anything. How fun is that? As you read this, you might be thinking it's silly or naïve and, if so, you are missing the point and are just making an excuse not to make your life better. What's so wrong with having a fun life? Nothing!

So, make it fun, but also make it count. Get what you really want out of life by simply defining it. Once you start to make the transition from a "don't want" to an actually "want", sit back and watch your life transform.

Love and a four leaf clover.

To paraphrase one of my favorite writers, "Look for love and you'll never find it. Stop looking and it will knock you down."

Isn't that true? The harder you look for love, the less likely you will find it. In fact, the harder you look for anything, the less likely you are to find it. When you look too hard, you usually overlook the very thing that you were searching for. And why is this? It's because you're too concentrated on the looking and not the finding. For instance, have you ever lost your keys? *But if I don't look for them, how can I ever hope to find them?* This is sort of where the Law of Attraction comes in.

We all want love. It's a human condition. We all want to be wanted. Ditto. However, sometimes we get everything a little messed up. We think we have to force something into action. We feel that if we don't try our hardest to do something, nothing will happen. And yet, it never happens anyway.

Strange, huh?

It seems as though the harder you work at something, the harder it is to obtain. Especially in matters concerning love. Just start looking for love—in all the wrong places, or otherwise—and you will never find it. Stop looking and it happens.

Why is this?

Because love, like anything else you really, really want in life, can only be found once you release. It's almost like you have to give up on it before it comes knocking at your door.

Have you ever really looked for a four-leaf clover? Once you try to find one, you will never do it. But once you stop, there's one, or two, or six. (I have found they usually grow in clusters.) You can't look too hard, you can't try too hard or you'll never find one. And that's the same deal with love.

Funny how that works.

But we think we have to control everything. Well, no we don't and we don't because we have the Law of Attraction. According to the Law of Attraction, whatever it is you want, you can have, simply by wanting it. Once you put the desire into the universe, it will be drawn back to you.

But why doesn't it always work? Like I said, it's because we work too hard, we're looking too hard for love or that four leaf clover. And we're looking too hard because we're trying to control the outcome. The magic is this: Let go of the outcome and watch whatever it is you desire happen.

Sometimes, we are our own worse enemies. We stand in our way of happiness and success, usually without even knowing it. We exhibit a needy, desperate attitude and once this happens, we start turning off guys we meet. Most people, men included, can smell desperation a mile away. However, when a girl is being desperate, she's rarely aware of it. But desperate we do become and when that happens, we block everything we want from coming into our lives, including love.

The good news is all you have to do to turn all this around is start having a positive, confident attitude. *Oh, is that all?* Listen, smarty pants, I am here to tell you if you want to turn your life around and start dating quality men, you have to have a good, positive attitude about it. Having a good, positive attitude may sound contrived, but it's the key component to getting the life you want and the man you want to date. Also, you have to know *what* you want, and most importantly, know that *you deserve it.* Once you can get in that mindset, the rest is cake.

Great concept, huh? Now go and see if you can find a four leaf clover by not really trying to find one and see how quickly it happens. And why will you be able to do this? Because you believe you can, but you're going to let go of the outcome. Once you let go you will find magical things begin to happen.

You have to want yourself.

You have to want yourself. Did you hear me? *You have to want yourself.* Yes, in order to be wanted, you have to first want yourself. Think about it before you roll your eyes. You have to like *you.* You have to enjoy being around you. If you don't enjoy your own company, how can you expect anyone else to? You can't and you shouldn't.

If you don't want yourself, who else is going to want you? This all goes along with the fear of rejection, of failure, which we will discuss a little later. We may feel it's best to sit home and not try, thereby letting life pass us by. But where will that get you? Sitting at home, alone, perhaps with a good bottle of wine, staring at the TV, looking forward to the new fall season and wondering why you feel just a little bit numb.

That doesn't sound like a fun life. But if you don't believe in yourself and you don't like yourself, this is probably something you will look forward to. But guess what? There's a whole world of living out there just waiting for you. *Yes there is!* All you have to do is *want* a better life, which will ensure that you get one. If you never want better, you won't get it. Remember, like attracts like.

But we have all been in a place in our lives where we've disliked ourselves. This is a common human condition. However, it's staying in that place for too long that can be detrimental to a happy existence. How do you change, then, and start to like—therefore, want—yourself? How do you get some self-esteem? You get it through doing things you *can* do and feeling proud about that, then you can feel good about other things you haven't tried yet, which will give you confidence to do more.

A good rule of thumb is this: Concentrate on what you can do, not what you can't do. Soon enough, you will realize there is more you can do than can't.

Everyone is afraid of doing anything because of the fear of criticism. "Oh, look at her; she's trying to get a good man. Who does she think she is?" What does it matter what they think? Forget them! Listening to others' criticism of you and taking it to heart will put you on a one-way street to disappointment in life. It's a shame, but women can be so mean to other women. When women don't do what they want in life and never get what they want, they turn mean and bitter. You can see this in many older women. They can be outright vicious! They make fun of women who actually try to look their best and don't become all sloppy and run-down like themselves. It is best to avoid these kinds of women, but it is *better* to not turn into them.

So, you might be afraid of what others will say about you doing something, but think of this: If you don't do anything, they'll talk about that too! So, you can't win! Most times, there's simply no pleasing anyone. So, how about this? Why not try to please yourself? And if you are the subject of gossip, wouldn't you rather them be gossiping about you doing something than not doing something? If you have the choice between pity and jealousy, take jealousy, every time.

I say we hold ourselves back from reaching our full potential. We settle for second best. "He doesn't have to call when he says he will—he's busy, after all." Why are we settling for this? Because we don't want ourselves, that's why and if we don't want ourselves, why would any man want us? Do you see what I'm getting at here? Well, you should.

So, you have to first want yourself before anyone will want you. You have to think you're the best. You have to know you are worth it. And how do you do this? Like I said, by building confidence in yourself. It's that easy. None of us think we're perfect, but that doesn't mean we're so imperfect we can't love ourselves. It just means we are human and we have the right to be wanted just like everyone else.

Some might say all this means is that you should love yourself. And, yes, you should. But, along with that love, you also need to enjoy your own company. If you don't enjoy being around yourself, who else will? No one!

The problem most of us have with wanting ourselves is we think it's a little too self-serving and maybe even a little weird. I am not saying, of course, to become a narcissist and stare at yourself in the mirror all day. I'm saying you have to want yourself before anyone else will want you. When you like yourself in this way, others will like you too.

When you want yourself, you don't make any excuses for the way you are or the way you dress or the way you look. You're just you and if no one else likes it, fine. However, exuding this self confidence is a good way to build relationships. People like being around people who are comfortable with themselves. Men especially like a woman who's comfortable in her own skin. This gives them the signal that she's someone who would be interesting to know more about.

So, I say, never apologize for who you are or what you want. Never apologize for your background, if you grew up poor or whatever. Never apologize for the size of your nose or body. Never, ever apologize for anything about yourself. You are all that you have. Honor that by loving and wanting yourself.

But what if you don't want yourself? How do you get to a place where you do? You just start accepting yourself little by little until you complete the whole package. You stop making excuses for yourself such as apologizing for the way you dress or look. If you are embarrassed by the way you dress, buy some new clothes that accentuate your body better. Hey, you deserve it! You can improve all areas of your life that you think you need improving on and this might give you the courage to improve the way you look at yourself. Change the way you look at yourself by accepting yourself and the rest will come easy.

Once you accept yourself for who you really are, you will see ways you can improve and that will improve the way others view you, too. Confidence really is everything, especially in dating, and the Law of Attraction won't work in your favor if you keep putting yourself down. It will, simply, give you more of what you're magnetizing back. But if you start thinking of yourself as worthy, as you should, that's what you'll get back—more feelings of being worthy. And so, soon, you shall be.

Cult of celebrity.

The Law of Attraction is nowhere in our universe exemplified better than it is with celebrities. We're jealous of them for a reason. They have it all! Why? Because they know they deserve their lives and don't allow guilt to step in and ruin it. Well, maybe some do, but those aren't the ones we're talking about.

Celebrities get what they want—fame, fortune, free cocktails—because they know what they want and they know they deserve it. Celebrities may be a little different from us in the way that they know what they want and have the ego not to let anyone tell them differently. Sounds like a great concept, huh? But many of us are afraid to do just that and allow our own insecurities to stand in the way of our success—from dating to finding a better job to just about anything.

But celebrities know what most of us don't—like attracts like. Take your favorite female celebrity—it doesn't matter who. What does she have? Is the best looking woman on earth? The smartest? The nicest? Probably a no to all three but she has something working in her favor and that something is the Law of Attraction.

Seriously though. Talent doesn't matter. How "good" you are doesn't matter. It's the Law of Attraction.

Why do some celebrities reach such heights when others falter? In my opinion, some are more in tune with the Law of Attraction than others. They might not know they are, but they are. The evidence is clear. They're lauded wherever they go, they get loads of swag and only have the best of everything.

Have you ever wondered how some actor got big? Whenever you watch this person on the screen, you think, "He's awful! Why is he a big star?" It's because he uses the Law of Attraction. He might not realize he's using it, but using it he is.

On the same side of a different coin, take the example of a bad movie, and we've all watched a few in our time. We've all watched some stupid movie that blew us away with its inanity. The thing is so over the top and so bad that you can't believe they actually paid someone to write it. And you wonder to yourself, "How did this get made? I could do a better job than that!" And you probably could. But that's not the point. The point is that this is the Law of Attraction in action.

Or have you ever wondered how some wormy guy ends up with the beautiful babe? It's the Law of Attraction. What the bad actor and the writer of that stupid movie and the wormy guy all have in common is that they have attracted their desires into their lives. They've manifested them via the Law of Attraction.

The great news is that none of us have to do without! There is plenty for everyone. Do celebrities do without? No. They take what they want and know that there's more where that came from. And that's all you have to do, too. Guilt might begin to play in your brain, making you think you don't deserve the greatness you're entitled to, but just stamp it out. You, too, can get what you want just like any celebrity. All you have to do is want it. That's the first step in a succession of steps that will bring you closer to the life you deserve.

Please release me.

I believe one of the things in life that many people get hung up on is releasing. What I mean by this is the fact that once any of us get started on anything, we think we have to follow it to the end and the end must conclude in the way we'd like. It's like we're saying, "I have to have this man, by this date and he has to take me to these restaurants and always show up with candy or flowers. If that doesn't happen, I won't have any of it." Do you see how constricted this is? It's full of control and some defiance. That's why, many times, we don't get what we want. We're trying to control the situation and once we do that, what we most want becomes almost impossible to attain.

One of the most important aspects of the Law of Attraction is release. Sure, state your desires but then release them. By releasing, you are allowing your desires to start turning into reality. You're not controlling them but rather allowing new ideas and possibilities to come into your life.

Release is nothing more than a way to uncomplicated what you want. Firstly, you have to figure out what it is you want and then, basically, not worry about it. In effect, once you figure it out, you just let it percolate and resolve itself while being outside of your control. To use a computer term, you just let your want run in the background while you work on other stuff.

But some of us just can't do it, can we? We're afraid to release. We can't let go of what we want. So, we hold onto it, so tightly, and squeeze it to death. However, this is just wrong. It is only by releasing will we ever get what we want. It's kind of like that saying, "If you love something, set it free. If it comes back to your, it's yours. If it doesn't, it never was."

But, like I said, we fear letting go because we don't want to lose control of anything. We get obsessed with what we want, how we'll get it and when. Then, when it inevitably doesn't appear because we haven't released, we get afraid it never will. This is why many women end up dateless on a Saturday night. That's why they don't have a special gift on Valentine's. It's not because they're undeserving; it's because they're trying to control every single thing that happens, which might be the reason they're not dating.

And yet, we can't let go: "But what if I release and it doesn't happen?" Well, what did you lose? Sleepless nights? Obsession? Just release. It's a win-win situation.

So, how do you release? Start living your life, that's how. Figure out what you want. Decide what sort of man you want to date and, quite possibly, marry. State your desires, and then release them. In the meanwhile, live your life. It's so simple, but we make it so difficult. When we don't release, we resist and resistance is nothing more than control. Let go of the outcome! In essence, you don't wait on it. You keep on truckin', but don't hold out until the big thing you've always wanted happens. If you wait on it, it's never likely to occur.

However, we all know that resistance is futile, or we should know that. And yet we are taught to resist what we don't want. "I don't want that job, apartment, boyfriend, car, dress, etc." And yet it persists. Carl Jung once said, "What we resist, persists." And wasn't he right? Whatever it is that we resist will always persist. Soon enough, our whole lives are comprised of what we don't want. This builds up so much resistance it's unbelievable. Then we have to make some changes. We have to start releasing in order to see any peace in our lives whatsoever. This is not a bad thing. It just means we're giving up control so we can be happier people.

Releasing not only works on what you want out of life, but when you're having trouble with something—or someone. There have been times in my life when things have been really difficult. Looking back, I can see that not releasing is where I made my mistake. Not letting go made things fester and, in the process, made me miserable. It was like I *could not* let it go. But, looking back, I realize now that all I had to do was let go and release. Once I began to make this a habit and not allow myself to obsess about things, I was a lot happier.

There have been other times in my life when I really wanted something. Again, it was like I just *could not* let it go. Whenever this would happen, it's like I'd get a little manic about it. *I have to have it—now!* But once I released, it usually just took place on its own. Seriously, when I push and tug at something, it never works. Never! I don't care how much effort I put into something, it simply won't work. But when I let go, it just seems to flow.

Yes, you do have to put in effort. You just don't have to kill yourself. You don't have to obsess or worry how it's going to happen. It will just take care of itself. All you have to do is have faith that it will happen, and so it shall. In a way, releasing is kind of like giving up on something. I have found that if I do this, I usually get what I want in some form. Funny how that works.

I believe that when you don't release, you're actually blocking whatever it is you want from happening because you're trying to control it. It's almost like you're always in a twist or in a strain. However, when you say, "I'm just not going to worry about it," you're letting it percolate. You're just not constantly thinking about it or obsessing. When you do this, you're releasing. Not worrying about it isn't failure, no matter what anyone says. Giving up is letting go, it's releasing. It's an important part of the process.

It's like this: We want something really badly, perhaps just a good date on a Saturday night. And we think about it so much, it begins to permeate our brains. We become obsessed. And by doing this, we're blocking it from happening, as I said previously. We're so obsessed that we don't recognize the opportunities and possibilities that life presents us with. This could happen by getting out and meeting people or going out on the town with your girlfriends, which could lead to seeing some random guy who catches your eye. He could be your Saturday night date! But if you think, "I'm just here with my friends," then you're not allowing it to happen. You're not recognizing that your desires might just be happening before your very eyes!

Things could start to happen if we just weren't so hung up on our idea of how something should happen. Not only that, we're miserable in the process! There's good news—we don't have to be miserable while we wait for our desires to surface!

But it's ingrained in us to not give up, to not let go, to persevere and work hard! But I ask you this: If perseverance and hard work pay off, why doesn't everyone get what they want? They're not letting go! They're not releasing.

The harder you try at something, the more likely you will fail. Believe me, I know. Doesn't it seem like it's almost like the more effort you put into it, the less you get out? The good news is, all you have to do is state your desires, live your life and when it happens, take action. You will know when it's happening, so don't worry. But trying to control the "if, when and how" of everything is nothing more than asking for it not to happen. So, release, let go and stop worrying about it! And watch your life transform before your very eyes.

The opposite of resistance is relief.

Once you begin to practice releasing and allow your desires to occur on their own, a wonderful thing happens—you begin to feel relief. And what a joy that is! It's so great not to tug and pull and push at everything. It's so good to get into the flow. And it's so easy how it works.

I'll give you an example. A good friend of mine needed a new car. The one she wanted was a little expensive but she really wanted *that* car. She'd pretty much given up on it, though. But one day, she was out walking when the idea of the new car occurred to her again. She thought, "I will go this weekend, look at this car and if the price is right, I will buy it." She didn't give it much thought after that, though. She went on with her life and whenever she thought about the new car, she'd smile thinking abut driving it, but didn't do much else. Over the weekend, she went to look at the car and, to her dismay, the price on the car was way over her budget. She was about to forget it all and get in her old car and leave when a salesman flagged her down and told her he could get her that car at a highly discounted price. She almost fell over! She wasn't so sure he was telling the truth, as it's hard to believe a car salesman, right? Yet, she waited for him to get the keys to the car, she test-drove it, fell in love with it, then followed him into the salesroom. They showed her the deal and it was still too high, so she left and ate lunch. Then she decided that if they brought the price down to an even lower price—which was so ridiculously low that she figured there was no way they would agree to it—then she would buy it. She went back and told them what she wanted. To her surprise, they agreed to her offer and she got the car she wanted at a steal. The salesman told her that one reason why she got such a good deal was because they really needed to liquidate their inventory and she'd arrived at exactly the right time.

How did she do it? She got into the flow. Getting into the flow is just allowing your wants to rise to the surface, feel them, then release them. It's just getting into the flow, that's all. And it works with anything you might want in your life. So, whether you're after a new car or a new man, it works the same. Release and feel the relief of not having to control everything and then welcome your wants into your life. You'll find things work out so much easier if you don't try so hard. The key is to know what you want in the first place, that way you recognize it when it comes along.

As I like to say, the opposite of resistance is release. And once you release something, you will have it. Like I said, it might not be in the neat little package you envisioned it in, but it will come, in one form or another.

So, once you learn how to release, you will feel the resistance fall away, and therefore, you will feel relief. This means good things can start happening.

You can't let him know how much you want him.

You can't let him know how much you want him. This is the single most important thing you will read in this book. It is *the* crucial element in being wanted. And with this, ladies, I am handing you the key to the kingdom. It's your choice to take it. What you do with it is at your discretion and always use with caution.

This simple rule is always overlooked by most women. Why is anybody's guess but I think they become so desperate they're going to lose a guy that they think they have to have him—at any cost. Which inevitably ensures their doom. You can't let him know how much you want him. You just can't! This is so important, I can't emphasize it enough. By knowing this and applying it, you can reach new heights in any relationship you might have in the future. With this rule, you are always in control and you always call the shots. With this rule, he has to chase you.

Keep in mind that the less he thinks you want him, the more he will want you.

But, for whatever reason, a lot of women just don't get this. And it sounds off, doesn't it? It sounds wrong. *If I like him and I don't let him know, then how will he know to come after me?* What you're forgetting is that he will come after you whether he knows you like him or not. In fact, I would venture to say, if he wants you, he will still come after you even if he thinks you *don't* want him. However, if you use this rule, you will up the ante.

It sounds almost counterintuitive but it's not. This is the Law of Attraction working in your favor with men. I'm not saying this will work in every case and with every man and in every situation. What I am saying is that it will work with most.

You might be thinking, "But you said all I had to do was want this guy and I'd get him and blah, blah, blah."

And that's what I say back: "Blah, blah, blah." Listen to me and listen carefully. You can't let a man know how much you want him—ever! If you do, he will run. I'm not saying you don't want him; I'm saying you can't let him *know* how much you want him. What's the harm in that? It will only benefit you to do this. There always has to be some measure of doubt in his mind about how much you want him. When this happens, he will want you more because you become more of a challenge.

Let's reiterate. Here is the trick, the secret, if you will, to being wanted: *You have to act as though you don't want him.*

I keep saying this because I really want it to sink in. You might still be thinking, "Huh?" Well, listen. When you find the man you want to date and, quite possibly, marry, you can't for a second let him know how much you want him. In fact, it's better to act as though you don't want him at all, at least in the beginning. Sure, over time, you can show him you think he's hot or whatever, but only after you know you've sealed the deal. Even then, coming off too strong might scare him off. You have to keep in mind that men like mystery and if you keep them guessing, you will become a mystery to them. But if you put it all out there, that doesn't leave that much for him to want to find out.

To put it in a cruder way: No one respects you if you kiss their ass. So, if you let some guy know you think he's the hottest thing since sliced bread, he's not going to respect you. Flattery is good, but with most men, it's not conducive to being wanted by them. No guy will appreciate it if you fall all over him. If you do this, it's almost like you're ingratiating yourself. Basically, you hold back, thus letting them come to you. And, because you will be applying the Law of Attraction, they *will* come to you, just because you put out that want.

Men can sometimes be like little kids. They want all the new games and toys, but once they get them, once they "master" them, they move into the next game or toy. You are not a toy or a game, but if you go ga-ga for him and let him know how ga-ga you are about him, he will think he's "mastered" you. And you become not so much fun after a while. And then he's ready to find a new toy or game.

In essence, you have to keep him guessing. *Does she like me or not? I sure do like her. But why does she act like she's not that into me? I don't get it.*

He might not get it, but you certainly will. Of course, this goes without saying, but I will say it anyway: Not letting him know how much you like him doesn't mean you have to act like you hate him. You just have to act not too interested.

You're probably still thinking, "But how will he know I like him if I don't act like I do?" It doesn't matter. The key is to not let him in on your desires because men don't like to be hunted. And if he thinks you've been hunting him, like a scared little bunny he's going to start feeling like he might get trapped and that means he will flee.

I've witnessed many a woman find a good man and then smother him. They buy him clothes, treat him like a king and, in the end, he runs off with the first bleached blonde he can find. Why? Because men, again, don't like to feel trapped.

On the other hand, I've witnessed many women who seem almost aloof with their men. They act as though they can take them or leave them. I have a good friend who's been married for years to a guy she can't stand. In fact, she acts like she almost hates him. You'd think he'd get the hint and leave, right? No. It makes him hang on tighter. Is it love? Perhaps. Most likely, it's the fact that people just can't stand it when they think someone doesn't want them and it makes them try that much harder to "get" that person to like them.

It might not make much sense at first, so sit with this for a bit and let it sink in. Take it or leave it, but this is the real secret to being wanted by men. If you go out to a club or bar or whatever, watch the men in there. They will make fools of themselves over women who won't give them a second glance. But the women who want to hang with them usually get ignored.

If you come on too strong, he's going to bail. It's that simple. Sure, at first, he might hang around if he's getting laid regularly. But he'll never respect, let alone, love you. It's a harsh reality and I wish it could be different because, at heart, I am a hopeless romantic. Maybe with some people it can be different, like in those romantic comedies. But in today's reality, men want variety and they also want to think they've got themselves a prize. If you act as though you're glad he's just giving you the time of day, that's all you'll ever get from him. But if you act like you're just giving *him* the time of day, he'll fawn over you. Which might get a little embarrassing. But, hey, it beats letting him in on what you're doing to keep him so smitten.

I will use an analogy here I am sure most of you will love. I call it "The Shoe Analogy". This whole thing can be likened to buying shoes, cheap shoes in fact. Cheap shoes might be easy to afford and look about as good as the more expensive kind, but most people don't go around dreaming about cheap shoes. Nor do they brag about them or keep them around for that long. They only do this with the harder to afford, less accessible expensive shoes. These are the shoes they are proud of and have a special shelf in their closets for.

You need to keep in mind that *you* are the expensive shoes. You are the shoes any guy will be proud to brag about to his friends. You are almost inaccessible. You are expensive. You are coveted. Once he gets his hands on these shoes, he will know he's got something great. But if you let him know how much you like him, you will become the cheap shoes he gets rid of after six months.

You might be thinking that this kinda, sorta goes against the Law of Attraction. But not really. What did we say earlier? Or, rather, what did Carl Jung say? *What you resist, persists.* If you resist him, he will persist. Bingo! This is why you will be irresistible to men.

While all this *is* about the Law of Attraction, this chapter is how you should conduct yourself in order to increase your possibilities with men. There are smart women out there who know this, understand it and always use it to get the man they want. Always! And if they don't? They usually end up with better. So be a smart woman, starting today!

The way I figured this out came quite accidentally. When I was younger and more naïve, I'd always let the guys I liked know I liked them. I'd send messages through my friends or whatever. And once I did that, whatever guy it was would inevitably end up ignoring me. Yes, this was quite embarrassing and I began to wonder what was wrong with me. I was attractive, in great shape and had a winning personality. (I'm not trying to be egotistical here; I'm trying to make a point, okay?) But these guys never liked me back. And what was funny was the fact that they always seems to show interest in me *before* I let them know how much I liked them.

This was very puzzling to such a young mind. What was I doing wrong? Was I ugly? Did I smell bad? Did they think something was wrong with me? And so, you see, I began to take it out on myself. I began to look down on myself, idiot that I was. There had to be something wrong with me if these guys didn't like me.

On the other side of this, however, were these boys I could not get rid of. They adored me. They really did! They bugged the crap out of me, called me at home to ask some stupid question, which was just an excuse for them to ask me out. They'd find ways to be in the same place as me so often they'd generally just drive me nuts. I wasn't much interested in them and told them so. *Leave me alone!* You'd think they'd get the hint, right? Wrong! I had to endure these guys who wanted me. Poor me, I know. Mostly, I ignored them and hoped they'd go away so I could concentrate on these other boys, whom I just couldn't figure out.

So, you can see my conundrum. Guys I liked didn't really seem to care for me. Guys I didn't like liked me. Huh. Interesting. One day, it just came to me. This was the Law of Attraction in action! I didn't want these guys to like me, but they did. And they liked me because I didn't like them. So, what if I just started acting like I didn't like these other guys? Would they come around to my side? Oh, yes, they would and they did. And that's the secret to being wanted.

This is the most important thing you will read in this book. It gives you a better chance with the guys you *really* want. I'd be willing to bet that if I'd just acted like I was interested in the guys who liked me, they would have run. So, on the other side of this, if you ever want to get rid of a guy just start to cling to him and let him know just how much you love him early on. He will flee—every single time! Just let him know how much you want him and he'll about break his neck getting away from you.

You might be thinking, "This is sort of high school-ish." Well, duh. Isn't that what the dating world is like? Go to any club and see the cliques. Another thought might be: "Isn't this a bit like being a maneater?" Well, duh again. Better to eat than be eaten, right? But kidding aside, doing this doesn't mean you have to turn into an actual maneater. It just means you get the man you want without expending too much effort. Haven't you always wondered how some women do it? I once overheard a conversation between two women. "I can't seem to ever get married. Men just don't want to marry women anymore," the first said. The second woman responded, with a laugh, "Girl, I've known women who've married six, eight times. Don't tell me men don't marry anymore."

So, what are these women's secret? How can some get married six, eight times while others can't manage to get married even once? They use the Law of Attraction and also, they're a bit maneater-ish. It's that simple. They might plow through the men to get the one they want, but they always have one. And they have one thing in common: They know men want women and they know *they* are wanted just by this fact and they use it. They're unafraid to get what they want. They never close themselves off to new possibilities, or new men. They know what they want—to have a man— and that's why they always get one. Or four.

The good thing about this is that it will be rare that you attract guys with low self esteem, i.e. guys with troubles. This is because only a guy with good self esteem will take the chance with you. Only these guys will have the balls to chase you, a girl who might just be out of their league.

I will end this chapter by this reiteration: Caution! Caution! Use this information with caution. When guys really fall for you, they will *really* fall for you. That means it will be hard to get rid of them. So be conscientious as you don't want to try it on some guy you don't really like just to see if it will work. Because, really, he's going to stick around until he gets you as long as he thinks you don't like him. And getting out of that tangled web might be more trouble than it's worth. So, always pick the best so you don't get stuck with the dud.

Forcing the issue.

I know some of you are still wondering, "But why can't I let him know how much I want him?" Therefore, I want to touch on this subject once more before we move on. I know a lot of women will read this bit of information and think I've lost my mind. I haven't. It's pretty simple stuff when you get right now to it.

You say, "But if he doesn't know about me, how will I ever get him?" The trick—faith! You will attract him by the Law of Attraction. In essence, you don't have to do any work. You just have to have faith that you will. Keep in mind that you can't force something to happen with a man. When you "have" to let him know how much you like him, you're trying to force him into dating you. This isn't going to look good, believe me. No one wants to be forced into anything.

So, say you want some guy and you let him know you want him. You bat your eyelashes at him and send him love notes and... Well, I don't think many of us would go that far, but you get the point. Whatever you do to let him know how much you want him will put him in the receiving end of a position he might not want. If he opens himself up to you in any way, he will be in a subordinate position, which means he might think he's being manipulated into making a decision about dating you. *You're forcing the issue*. So, when you back off in this way, it's up to him to figure you out. It's up to him to get the ball rolling and, more importantly, keep it rolling.

However, if you persist, he will become more and more uncomfortable, thereby resisting. It's almost if you let him know how much you want him, you're forcing him to make a decision. This makes him figuratively curl up into a fetal position. If you think about it, we all do this. (Maybe men more than women, but still.) Anytime someone wants us to do something really, really bad, it makes us slightly uncomfortable and we back away. Now, when a woman does this to a man, he realizes how totally *not* in control he is and this makes him want to run. He doesn't want to be forced into anything. If you do somehow force him, and he caves, he'll think, "The next thing I know, she'll have me married with five kids, two dogs and a mortgage." This frightens some men.

So, all you have to do is ease up a little. You just have to take a breath and let him do all the work, which is what he's supposed to do anyway. Just because you don't wave big poster boards in front of him to let him know he's what you want doesn't mean he won't get the hint. Subtlety is everything.

I know you're still thinking, "But how do I let him know I want him? If he doesn't know, he won't pursue me." This just isn't true. You've had guys pursue you that you didn't want before, haven't you? And how did you do that? Just by being your cute little self, right? It's the same thing, only in reverse.

And here's where the Law of Attraction comes in. What you have to do is—nothing! That's right. Just state your desire and then release it, just like I've been saying. This is the beauty of the Law of Attraction. All you have to do is sit back and wait for your desires to materialize. And, because you know what you want, you'll recognize when the possibilities present themselves.

Sure, you can ask him out on a date. Why not? I've seem many women do it and with good results. I, personally, don't think there's anything wrong with it. However, only do it if you think it's absolutely necessary. And when you do it, just ask him for coffee or drinks. And then see where it leads.

However, I think if you just give him time, he'll come to you. *Just allow it to come about.* When you look at it this way, it's almost redundant to try to force anything to happen. It will happen or it won't. Either way, you don't end up with egg on your face. And you don't have to look like some crazy, obsessed chick. All you have to do is sit back, relax and allow it to happen. Not a bad trade-off, in my opinion.

Everything you know might quite possibly be wrong.

Everything you know might quite possibly be wrong. It's true. Everything you know, at least about men and getting what you want out of life, might be wrong. That's why when you become familiar with the Law of Attraction you might think, "This just doesn't make sense to me. It sounds *too* easy."

Oh, ye of little faith.

We've all been taught that if something is too easy, then it's too good to be true. Don't fault your parents if they taught you this. Mine taught me this, too. They taught me that life is hard. Work hard. Keep your head down. All that crap. And you know what? They were right. And why were they right? Because I believed them. For a long time, I believed that life was hard and I had to work hard to get anything out of life. And, therefore, I attracted a hard life.

This went on for a while too. I'd toil away at my job, which I hated with a passion. But I'd dream, too. No, no, they couldn't take away my dreams. In my fantasy world, I didn't have it that bad. In fact, I had a pretty cool beach house and loads of money and good friends. Real life wasn't that great, but living in fantasy land was terrific.

But soon, fantasy land was bombed by reality and I found myself living in a painful world. Fear began to take root in my life. Friends I'd once loved fell by the wayside. Things weren't so peachy. But what could I do about it? Life was hard, that's what I'd been taught. Suffering is inevitable. I couldn't quit my job and pursue my passion. I certainly couldn't follow my bliss. That was for other people. Better people than me.

But then, something happened. I didn't start reading about the Law of Attraction until later. In fact, I was so stuck in not-so-peachy land, I don't know how this glimmer of sunshine came into my life. But, anyway, one day, I realized that I didn't have to follow the status quo. I could do what I wanted to do. I could have the relationships I wanted. All I had to do in order to obtain these things was get through this cobbled mess of my life. And that meant I had to get over the idea that was instilled in me about working hard and keeping your head down and all that other crap.

You see, my vision of what I wanted my life to be was born in fantasy land. If you dream it, you can do it. *Just use your imagination.* That's what I had to do in order to get where I wanted to go in life. And that's what I did. I decided I couldn't take it anymore and got up the guts and started my own business. And—guess what?—I'm now much happier. I work my own hours and I do pretty much what I want to. My family is slack-jawed at what I've created. And guess what? If I had listened to them, I'd still be working a crummy job for crummy pay and hanging out with people who undermined me.

However, as I did this, I still had doubt. *Why am I so unique that I get to do what I want in life? What makes me so damn special? I don't deserve this, do I?* Well, guess what? That fear crept in and soon I began having anxiety. I'd worry about this and I'd worry about that, all because I believed I was doing something wrong by living my life the way I wanted to live it! In essence, I began to undermine myself. But we do what we've been taught to do.

Like attracts like. The more I worried, the more I had to worry about. It got so bad, I felt light-headed and miserable most of the time. One day, I just began to pray to God. I asked for strength and I asked for something good to come into my life. And soon, thereafter, it did. And after that, I discovered the Law of Attraction. And after that, I realized that everything I knew was wrong.

The hardest thing for me was getting over what I'd been taught by my parents and my teachers and my religious leaders. But then again, maybe they were just teaching me what they'd been taught, even if it was wrong. I do sometimes wonder why no one ever questions anything. Why is there so much misery in the world? Why so much suffering? Are we bringing it onto ourselves? Quite frankly, yes. I did. I didn't have to be miserable for a minute. And neither do you. It's just that we've been taught we have to suffer. We've been taught that life is hard. And, I'll say it again, like attracts like. If you believe that life is hard, then life *will be* hard.

So, do you want it to get easier?

The power of negative thinking.

This is a take on the old "power of positive thinking", but in reverse. We all know that the more positive you are about things, the better things are. And we *should* know that the more negative we are about things, the worse they will be.

Negativity will zap your soul. In fact, it will suck every bit of joy out of your life. You might not be a negative person, but have you ever been around one? It's soul crushing—literally. Negative people are like emotional vampires. If you're around one long enough, you will start to wonder if there really is any good in the world and only recognize the bad.

Time and time again we choose negativity. Why? Because negativity takes the blame off us. It takes the responsibility off us too. We're victims! This was done to us! If only it were that easy.

Negativity is nothing more than a habit. It's so easy to be negative and also somewhat fun, although in a twisted way. It's fun to make fun of things as we appear super cool, isn't it? It's so fun to look down our noses and shake our heads in pity at others. It's fun until it starts to affect your brain and soon enough, it will.

Have you ever noticed how when you start talking negatively about something, everyone chimes in with more negativity? And how eventually it gets to the point that it seems almost inappropriate to say or view the situation positively? And the situation then gets even worse. This is the Law of Attraction. Negativity breeds negativity. The same principle applies to everything in life.

So, if we know this, why do we do it? Think about it. It takes just as much energy to be negative—maybe more—than to be positive. So why do we chose negativity? Like I said, it becomes a habit and once you get into the habit of negativity, you are going to be on the losing end of everything. Nothing will ever be good enough and nothing will ever seem fun again.

If you've found yourself in this habit, why not just stop? And it's easy to do this. All you have to do is start looking at things differently and you do that by changing your perspective. Instead of turning your nose at everything, stop every once in a while and smell the roses. I mean it, too. Stop in the market and smell the roses. And now, build on that. Be nice to your neighbors instead of running from them. Don't engage in negativity with your friends, either and if all your friends are profoundly negative—and these types tend to run in packs—it might be time to look for new friends.

The point is that the Law of Attraction does work—like attracts like. And if you are ensconced in negativity, that's all you'll get back—more negativity. But if you're tired of it and want a better life, just stop. Look on the bright side of things, stop making fun of others and don't hang around people who roll their eyes at others' happiness.

It's one thing to be cool. It's quite another to be super negative. The Law of Attraction probably won't ever bring you what you want if negativity has permeated your life. Getting a really good man to date and maybe marry will be harder the more negative you are. Because, if you want a really good man, a good man is rarely a negative person, so even if he was attracted to you at first, once he gets a whiff of your negativity, he's going to bail. And, like I said, negativity is just a habit and it's one that can be broken, if you take the time to start breaking it.

Never chase a man.

Never chase a man. That's it. Never—ever!—chase a man. No matter how good looking he is, no matter how rich he is, no matter how much you want him. Just *don't* do it. Because, once you start running after him, he'll start running in the other direction.

For some reason, this bit of information escapes many women. But it makes complete and total sense. Men don't like to be chased. I don't care what any of them say, they don't like to be chased. They like to chase. It is in their genetic makeup. It's their job. If you chase him, you're not letting him do his job and this dis-empowers him. And he won't like that much and he'll start running away.

The problem some women have is that they think once they find that one good man, they *have* to have him. If they let him escape, there might not be another one. I say this is complete and total nonsense. You might be thinking, *But where are the men?* They're everywhere. Keep in mind that there is plenty to go around for everyone. There is an abundance of men. Don't ever think that all the good ones are taken because they're not.

There are more single people than ever but they have one thing on common—they all want to date someone. Eventually, most want to get married. This means, if this is want you want too, you will attract someone who wants the same thing you do. It's the Law of Attraction in action. All you have to do is wait it out a bit and watch it appear. That's all! You don't have to push and you don't have to prod but you do have to have a little bit of patience. Just know what you want that way you recognize it when it presents itself to you.

The point is to not worry so much about how you're going to meet someone, or really go after him once you do meet him. The point is to get you to the place where you're *ready* to meet someone. Once you're ready, you will be alert and when it happens, you will *know* it is happening. This lets you completely and totally off the hook as far as chasing a man. He's the one who's supposed to chase. So let him do his job. You just sit back and watch the show. I am more than sure it will be entertaining.

What's your inspiration?

A beautiful wedding dress? A baby? To have your girlfriends be envious? Something to do on a Saturday night? Someone to read the Sunday paper with? Whatever it is, let it guide you to the life you want.

Your inspiration could be anything. It doesn't matter. What matters is that it *inspires* you to take action to manifest your desires. I know a lot of people have a hard time doing this just because they think if they want something "too" badly, they won't get anything at all. This is hogwash. You can have anything and everything you want. All you have to do is want it.

So, what's your inspiration? What are your dreams? I know as you read this, you might think this seems a little hokey. It sounds so trite, so talk-show-ish, doesn't it? But it works. Believe me, it works. All you have to do is be willing to believe you can and will get anything you want in life.

If you're unsure of what you want exactly, sit down with a few magazines. They could be any kind, too. If you desire a beautiful house, sit down with some home magazines or furniture catalogues from your favorite—and, perhaps, most expensive?—retailers. You could look at some celebrity magazines or beauty magazines. As you flip the pages, pick out the things you like or the lifestyles that appeal to you and say to yourself, "Yes, that inspires me. I want that!"

Also, why not check out some of the good looking men in those magazines? Even if you're more into the intellectual sort, there are lots of magazines about technical stuff and science where you can learn more about the type of man you'd like to meet.

Another good thing to do in order to get your inspiration pumping is to create vision boards. I know this might seem like something only a teenage girl would do, but it works. This is also a good way to figure out what you want. If you're unsure of what a vision board is, it's just a big board—you could use a poster board, a magnetic chalk board or a corkboard—where you place images from magazines of things you want to attain in your life. You can also change the things around from time to time as well as put some cute guys on those boards. Why not? Additionally, you can write out what you want on the board.

If this seems like it might be a recipe for future embarrassment if someone in your life ran across your vision board, just know that you don't have to tell anyone you're doing it. But if you'd rather be more discreet, you can get a notebook and paste your favorite images in it. You can put it away where no one will see. It doesn't matter. As long as you have it is all that counts.

Teenage girls always do this, but they take it overboard. Go into any one of their rooms and you will see images from magazines and posters plastered all over their walls. They never leave a space uncovered. However, don't dismiss them so easily. *They get it.* They're envisioning their future! I know I did it. I bet you did, too. The reason we stop doing this is because we begin to think it's silly, that someone might make fun of us for doing it. We just get beaten down by life and think that it's impossible to get what we really want. But if we want to get what we want out of life, this is a great place to start. It can help you figure out exactly what you want.

As you work on your vision board, your mind will begin to open up to all the possibilities. Be sure that you don't limit yourself, either. If you want it, post it. This is a wonderful process and shouldn't be discounted. It may take you some time to get things in order, but take that time to do it.

The inevitable question.

You might be thinking to yourself, "Well, all this is all well and good but what does it have to do with getting a man?" And to that I say, "Everything!" (I covered this briefly in the first chapter.)

By using the Law of Attraction, you can pretty much do anything and that includes getting a good man. The thing to keep in mind is that this covers all aspects of your life. You just have to get to the point where you believe in yourself enough to go through with whatever it is you want to do. In order to take action, you must first believe in yourself and the better-rounded you become, the easier that will be.

So, another inevitable question might be: What do you have to lose? The greatest minds in history have used the Law of Attraction. So, what makes you think it won't work for you? Keep in mind that almost all successful people are successful because they started out knowing what they wanted. If you know what you want, you can have it. And what most women want is a good man to date and, quite possibly, marry.

But one of the main reasons many women don't get the man or the life they want is because they start out thinking that they can't have a good man or a good life. It's like it's almost ingrained in them to always take less and to expect less. And we all know that like attracts like. Expecting less means you will end up getting less.

I know a lot of people wouldn't even embark on this sort of thing, mainly because they will find an excuse not to. All that means is that they don't have faith that things will work out to their advantage. What a sad way to live life.

If you want something, you can have it. It's that simple. If you want a good man, you can have him. So, what do you have to lose by believing that the Law of Attraction can bring everything you've ever wanted into your life? I'd have to say you don't have anything to lose, except maybe your misery.

But I don't wanna...

Don't focus on what you don't want. Let me tell you if you focus on what you don't want, that's what you'll get—a whole bunch of don't.

Starting now, begin to focusing on what you do want. From now on, only focus on what you do what. Put the "don't" aside—banish it! One way we keep ourselves from happiness is focusing on what we don't want. We do this constantly and soon it becomes part of the daily jargon that goes on inside our heads. "I don't want another cold sandwich from that deli." Or, "I don't want to be late." Perhaps, "I don't want to date another loser!"

Get it? By only telling ourselves what we don't want, we're focusing too much on the negative aspect of a want, and not enough on the positive. Instead, you could say, "I want a delicious sandwich today." Or, "I want to be on time." Perhaps, "I want to date a man of substance."

In effect, if you're always focusing on not wanting the cold sandwich, you're always looking for the cold sandwich. If you start looking for the delicious sandwich, you're much more likely to find it and know it when you see it. Same goes for men. If you're always focused on not dating a loser, that's all you'll pretty much find. However, if you start focusing on a good man, you're more like to find him.

You see, if we only focus on what we don't want, that's all we'll ever get. According to the Law of Attraction, we will get what we focus on most, even if it is negative. The

Law of Attraction brings what we focus on back to us in abundance. So all your "don'ts" become a reality, a part of your day to day living.

And yet, this isn't all bad. You can use your "don'ts" for greater good. As I mentioned, having a "don't" is a good place to start to recognize what you don't want. There are so many things in our lives we don't want, from getting stuck in traffic to dating horrible men to living in crappy apartments. Sure, we know what we don't want. That's easy, right?

Another good way to use the "don't" to your benefit is to realize a "don't" might just be leading you in the direction you want to go. Mostly, you just have to turn it around. So, "I don't want to date another cheater!" could mean that you *do* want to date a loyal guy who won't cheat. "I don't want to gain any more weight!" could just mean you want to lose the excess pounds you've accumulated. Therefore, just turn it around, "I want to lose these extra pounds."

So, sit down and write out every single thing you don't want in you life. This may take days. It may take weeks. Who knows? But focus on it and get it out of your system once and for all. This is a great way to purge all your "don'ts". Once you are done, you can put your "don'ts" away for good. Now that you have it out of your system, begin to think about what you *do* want in your life. Once you start doing this, you can always take the "don't" out of the equation.

So, the "don'ts" are easy to correct. You just have to be conscious of when you're enabling a "don't" to become a reality in your life. And all you have to do is focus on what you do want and not what you don't. The side effect of this is that it changes your perspective on life and will make you generally feel better about everything.

Are you governed by fear?

Everyone is afraid of something. Many women are afraid they will never find "the one" and they'll miss out on that part of life which is so important. Or, at the very least, some really good sex. Having fear is normal, especially in dating matters. It's how you deal with it that counts.

I think one of the main problems that keep people from their bliss or desires or whatever name you want to put on your true wants is fear. Sure, as you get older, fear tends to creep in because you begin to see that time is wasting and, soon enough, you feel that the window of opportunity to find a good man is closing. That would scare the bejesus out of anyone! What to do? Get over it! The best way to get over any fear you have is to just do what you fear most and what most of us fear is failure.

But one of the main causes of fear, in my opinion, is what I like to call "the incident". We've all had something that's happened to us in our past that's marked us—the incident, if you will. Either it's a betrayal of some sort or something stepped in our way of getting what we wanted out of life or whatever. After that, we turn indifferent and old—or at lease we begin to feel this way, when before we were young and happy and full of life. It's like you're going along, thinking everything will turn out okay, then boom! Life isn't so fun and exciting anymore. In fact, it's a little scary. *What if they're right? What if I can't do what I want? What if I can't find my man? What if I never get my white picket fence? What if the incident that has occurred in my life means that I am just undeserving?* Everything shifts and panic sets in. The world suddenly seems cold and uncaring. And this is because we've let this one incident take over our beliefs. And, therefore, we've started to become governed by fear and when this happens, we deaden ourselves so that we won't be hurt again.

This isn't much fun.

The next step is to start questioning yourself. I like to call this the "what if-ing". *What if it doesn't come? What if I try and I get rejected? What if I believe in this and it never happens? What if I've worked this hard and don't get anything in return? What if no man ever finds me desirable?* I could go on and on but I think you get my point. All the "what if-ing" is just plain old fear. It's just fear! Any "what if" question usually has fear behind it.

Sure, you may put yourself out there and get rejected. That is a possibility. Risk *is* involved but so what? Everyday we live with risk and we're usually okay, right? Apply that to anything and walk through the fear. Unless you place an action behind a desire, you're going to end up with squat. And you deserve better than that.

Some common fears:
- Fear of rejection. (Men not digging you.)
- Fear of failure. (Not getting married, not having kids, etc.)
- Fear of disapproval. (From parents, friends, etc. about the type of men you date.)
- Fear of disappointment. (From the men you date, i.e., he doesn't measure up in some way.)
- Fear of getting older. (Not finding "the one" before you turn forty or whatever.)

- Fear of uncertainly. (Not sure what the future hold for you, if anything.)

We fear rejection because we don't want to be humiliated. If we put ourselves out there and we get rejected, it's very humiliating, isn't it? That's not fun. It makes us feel bad, so not trying becomes our mantra just because we fear abject humiliation.

We fear failure so we stop ourselves from even trying. However, without trying, we will inevitably fail. Kinda like a Catch-22, isn't it?

We fear disapproval because we want approval from others. To be accepted is a very human need. We all need that and without approval, life can be tough.

We fear disappointment because it's hard to try and do something and never get to go through with it. It's better to just not try and not feel that inevitable disappointment. One reason we stop hoping and wishing and wanting a better future is because we have this fear of disappointment. We're afraid to state our desires because it might just not happen. This closes us off to anything good and new entering our lives. And we get pretty much the same bland existence we've tried so hard to avoid.

We fear getting older because we stop seeing the possibilities and hope for the future. The fun and enjoyment for life just seems to vanish.

We fear uncertainty because we want life to come in a nice, little package. We want to be certain of something happening. However, we can never be certain of anything. If we knew everything that was going to happen, life would be a bore.

And, as we fear all these things… Well, fear sets in. And once fear takes root, it's hard to weed out the good from the bad. But how do we stop all these fears from sucking the joy out of life? Easy. Start wanting what you really want out of life and then take action when know what you want is happening. That's it.

None of us know what's going to happen. A good looking guy could move in next door to you. In this case, uncertainty isn't a bad thing. It's exciting! Think of all the possibilities!

If you don't feel wanted in life—this is a fear—any decision you make will torment you. You will always doubt yourself. *Should I or shouldn't I quit my job? Should I marry this one or that one? Should I buy a new car? Should I go see my mother this weekend, even though I want to do other things?*

And this goes on and on until you become so encumbered with the fear of making a mistake, you can't do anything. You have "what if-ed" yourself to death! It might even be tough to leave your house! Yeah, it can get that bad. So, don't let it! Take control right now. Get over these very common fears and find your solid ground. Walk on that solid ground every day by believing in yourself and believing you deserve what you want out of life. And you know what? You do deserve everything you want out of life. Why? There's no reason why! Just because you're human, that's why. Every human on this earth deserves good things in their lives and every woman deserves a good man. But it is up to each of us to manifest our desires. And you can do that, starting right now by getting over your fears.

Keep in mind that if you never try, you've failed before you even start. In fact, you just failed at getting started. So, avoiding doing something because you're afraid of failure means you will never accomplish anything. So, in actuality, you're avoiding nothing. Except, maybe, the possibility of success.

So what else can you do? You can grow a backbone and start standing up for yourself. You can start believing. *Decide* what you want out of life and then go for it. Don't hesitate. Keep in mind that you're not only opening your heart but your mind as well. This could take some time, but invest in that time and see your life change dramatically. Soon enough, you will look back at all your fears and laugh. And, boy, does that feel good.

Want vs. need.

At the beginning of the book, I spoke briefly about how everything is about being wanted. We all know the old saying, "You can't get what you want, but you can usually get what you need." I don't believe this is true at all and that's because I believe when you place a need before a want, you're setting yourself up for failure.

Dating, unfortunately, can sometimes be a very needy activity. People who are out there "on the scene" can sometimes give off the vibe of neediness. Just go to a bar sometime during happy hour and observe the neediness, especially from the men. Bars can sometimes be the saddest place on earth. However, we all do "need" someone in our lives, someone who will want us, who will protect us, who will buy us jewelry. Well, okay, maybe not the last need, but you get my point. We do need other people in our lives and, as women, we especially need men.

However, it shouldn't really be this way. Whenever we put need before want, we tend to take less from life.

When you come from a place of need, as in you *need* to be wanted, any rejection or loss is devastating. If you have a secret belief that no one really wants you, you will do anything in your power to get your needs met. You might be the one who always pays for lunch. You might be the one who shows up on time when everyone else is late. You might let guys walk all over you. You might just take a lot of crap from people. And why do you do these things? It's all because you're afraid no one will like you.

Like I've said, we've all had "the incident" happen to us that zaps our confidence. We go from wanting to be liked, to *needing* to be liked—big difference! And then we begin to overcompensate. When we overcompensate, we start to become really nice to everyone we meet, hoping that by showing how nice we are, everyone will like us and invite us to join in. In a perfect world, everyone would find this refreshing. *She's so nice!* However, we do not live in a perfect world and when you're a little too nice, people tend to get a little suspicious. Therefore, niceness can be viewed as being a weakness. It's sad, but true. This might be the reason why you sometimes wonder, "If I'm so nice, then why isn't anyone being that nice to me?" This isn't a fun position to find yourself in. It feels like you're the only one who didn't get invited to the party, right?

So, once this happens, we get desperate. Now you do *need* it—that approval—to regain the confidence you lost. You feel off-kilter, right? Things just aren't right with you since this happened. And that's because you're coming from a place a need. This doesn't mean, of course, that you should turn cold and mean. You can still be nice, just don't be overly nice. Being overly nice sends out red flags.

I don't believe that the world responds well to needy and desperate but, sometimes, we find ourselves in this very position. Along with this, we begin to feel all sorts of "bad" feelings—frustration, anger, etc. and this just exacerbates the situation. Then we *need* something to happen to make us feel better. *I need a good man in my life—pronto!* If we don't have it—or him—soon, we'll feel terrible. We're just trying to get back to the place of feeling okay.

So, what can you do? You have to play it cool. I believe the world responds well to strong-willed, confident individuals. Aren't those the kind of people you want to hang out with and emulate? Sure, most of us do. Again—*you have to play it cool.* Otherwise you come off as being needy and desperate and that's a red flag to anyone you might meet. Have you ever needed a job? Well, you finally get the interview and you go in with that need. *I need this job—now!* You might go as far to say that to your potential employer. This is going to make them uncomfortable and they're going to look at you as somewhat desperate. And if they think you desperately need the company you're applying for to make your life better, rather than being a productive employee, they might just pass on your resume. This person is just interviewing you for a job. He or she doesn't want to be the one person who makes or breaks you.

Or, you might be unlucky enough to come across someone who takes your need and uses it to their advantage. You might get a boss who thinks you need the job so badly that they pile extra work on you and make you work late every day. You might get a man who thinks you need him so badly that he can treat you anyway he wants by not calling, showing up late and, quite possibly, cheating on you. You might get a friend who knows you need them more than they need you and start treating you awful and never reciprocating for lunch or dinner or whatever. They might be the ones who never call and ask you out to the movies. It might always be you and because you need them more than they need you, they get to call all the shots. Don't be surprised when you find out they've been hanging out with *other* friends and not inviting you along.

Do you get it? If you come off as needy, you can never truly be wanted for who you are. Your needs will overshadow everything about you, from your looks to your personality. Coming from a place of need puts you in a lower position. And, sometimes, people will take advantage of this. Other times, they'll just try to stay as far away from you as possible. Being in need equals being desperate. And coming off as desperate is never a good look for anyone.

But what can you do to get out of this very awkward position? Like I said, you have to play it cool. You have to act like you take it or leave it. It's the same thing with men. If you come off as being needy and desperate, they're going to run. At first, men are just in it for a good time. If you act like you need them, it makes them feel responsible for you in some way. Not a pleasant way to start off a relationship, right?

Here's a really good way to look at it: If no one ever invites you to a party, why not have your own party? That way, you don't have to wait for others to ask you to join in, they have to ask you. It totally switches things up. Of course, I'm not talking about an actual party, though throwing a party is rarely a bad idea, I'm talking about the party of *life*. Once you learn to play it cool, to step back and let things come to you, you might find yourself getting asked to join the party more. And the party could just be dates or barbeques. It doesn't matter. Playing it cool keeps you looking cool, believe me. And once you start having fun on your own without depending on anyone else, others will want to know what's up with you.

So, you have to relax enough to let go and by doing that, you're saying, "I can take it or leave it." And then be willing to do just that. When you let go in this way, you're paving the way for a better future and your "now" isn't so bad either. By doing this, you're enabling yourself to relax and just go with the flow. You're not forcing things but rather allowing them to happen. Once you get into the flow, everything should take care of itself. *But you have to let go.* You might not get *this* man or *this* job, but, by being willing to let go of them, you might get something or someone better in the future.

You are in charge.

You are in charge. I'm not talking in the bedroom either—that's a whole 'nother subject for a whole 'nother book. I'm talking about your being in charge of the relationship before it begins. In fact, you are in charge of whether the relationship even starts. It is all up to you and if you will just begin to realize this, you will be totally in control.

But how is this? How can I be in charge if the guy is the one who's supposed to ask me out and all that? If this is your question, then you are totally missing the point. When a woman allows a guy to think that he's in charge from the get-go, she may find herself being walked over. Some guys will take advantage of this. If this happens, you might find yourself in a relationship with a guy who has a mindset of someone from the 1950s. And I don't see you baking cookies in your housecoat anytime soon.

The main point of this chapter is this: You have to treat men a little like they should be happy you're taking the time. And by this I mean, treat all men you date like this, even the ones you really, really want. Never fall all over them. In a way, you have to treat men like you're deigning to go out with them. Like he should be glad you're taking the time. This doesn't mean to go overboard and act like a snooty bitch. No, no, no. This means, you're busy, too, and you have a lot going on. So he should be glad you're taking the time. He should be glad you're going out with him, not the other way around. By thinking this way, this lends itself to you being in charge.

Of course, you should feel this way anyway. Men today don't have to do squat to get women. Don't be like everyone else and just do whatever they want you to do. You are in control and until you realize it, you will end up looking like you're glad *he* took the time. This will not put you in a position of being wanted anytime soon.

Obviously, there is a fine line you must walk when you're in charge because you can't really let the man think you're in charge. He has to think *he* is. So, what you have to use the power of suggestion. Once you find a man you would like to date, all you have to do is to suggest what you'd like to do. He can veto it, of course, but he won't. This allows him to think that while his idea might be good, yours might be better.

Also by occasionally holding out on him and not going out with him whenever he wants will make him want you even more. By using some control in this way, you show him you have a lot going on and that you're being nice by going out with him. This puts him in a position where he starts to see the value of you, and the value of a future relationship, as well.

This also comes into play when the sex issue comes up. When should you give it up? How soon? In my opinion, it doesn't matter. However, it *will* matter to him. If you give it up too soon, he'll have what he wants and he might just fly like a bird right out of your life. Men see women as conquests and, until you can lay that groundwork of him falling in love with you, it might be a good idea to refrain from sex. If he sees you as an easy conquest, the challenge of "getting you" won't keep him interested long enough to get to know the actual you. Therefore, if he can't get to know you, he probably won't fall in love.

However, if you stay in control of these things, he will stick around to see what's up with you. But you have to walk a fine line. If you get too controlling, that's exactly what he'll think of you. He will think you're a controlling bitch he'd rather not fool with. However, if you go with the flow and don't try to control every little thing, he will get really relaxed.

Of course, this sounds like I'm talking out both sides of my mouth, but I want to get my point across. You have to stay in control and by that I mean, don't let him know too soon about how you feel. Also, you can make suggestions but go along with him from time to time to show that you're not *that* in control and it doesn't matter that much to you. (And, really, where you eat or what movie you see shouldn't be that big of a deal.) When it comes to sex, later is always better than sooner so you can lay the groundwork of a relationship. And he will never suspect a thing.

Genie in a bottle.

There is a difference between wishful thinking and actually stating what you want out of life. The difference is minute and I think a lot of people get hung up here. I also think it needs a teensy little explanation. So, if you're still unsure of how all this works, let me put it in simpler terms by using the Genie in a bottle scenario.

"Your wish is my command," the Genie says. So, when the Genie asks what your wish is, what are you going to say? You're *not* going to say, "I wish I had a pony" or whatever it is. You're going to say, "I *want* a pony."

And that's the difference between wishful thinking and stating what you want. Instead of saying, "Damn, I wish I had a good man!" you would say, "I want a good man!" If you wish for something, it might not happen. (I think they call it wishful thinking for a reason.) But if you actually *want* something, it probably will. You don't wish to do something. You want to do it: "I want…" That's why it's so important to *state* your desire and put it in the present tense. Wishing for something is all well and good, but that's all you'll ever be doing—wishing. But stating something as fact, actually *wanting* it into existence, stands a better chance happening. So, bringing that man you want into your life actually has a better chance of occurring. Otherwise, you might just be wishfully thinking, "I wish I had a good man." That sounds kind of needy, doesn't it? I can just see the dour looks on faces as they make this statement. "I wish I had a good man, but, poor me, I'll never have one." No! Want a good man and then get yourself one: "I want a good man!"

That's what we're after. And state what you want. And, more importantely, make the *decision* to go for it. I know as some people read this, negative thoughts will enter into their minds and they'll think, "Careful what you wish for, it might just come true." That's called superstition. Obviously, you want to use this for good, to better your life. You don't want to bring harm to any other human being. So, I say, only *want* with good intentions. Want things that will bring happiness to your life. And the negative thoughts? They're usually just in your head anyway, right? Sure, they are. We all have negative thoughts. And you can override them at any time. They're probably the reason most of us live with so much self-doubt. And that's no way to live.

The comfort zone.

The day inevitably comes when every one of us must spread our wings and fly. A time when we must embrace our destiny and never look back. However, for some, this time is approached with great trepidation and a little unease.

Sure, you want more out of life, you want *better*. The thought of dating some really great guy is enticing. Every girl wants that. Getting there might not be the problem; it's getting the moxy to actually go after a better life that might be scary. This comes about because we get into the comfort zone. What this means is simple. This means that we've become complacent, comfortable. Looking ahead into the future and envisioning a better life can be scary. It can be scary to start the hunt for a new man. But this doesn't mean you shouldn't. It just means you're human and sometimes humans need a little prodding to get going.

The ironic problem with comfort zones is that in reality they are usually very uncomfortable. I know when I was in mine, I hated almost everything about my life, but I had a fear that if I moved forward, I might just get slapped down. Even after I took a chance and quit my job and started my new life, my father told me, "You'd better get a job." Talk about un-positive reinforcement! Here I was, starting a new life, which was giving me anxiety to begin with because it was, in fact, so new, and my own father didn't have any faith in me. He was a nay-sayer! Maybe he was worried, so did that mean *I* should be worried? Was I going to starve to death? Was I stupid for quitting my job? Oh, my God! What was going to happen to me?

I'll tell you. I went through with my new life and have never regretted it. What I regret is allowing fear to take over for a while and make me miserable. Oh, if I could do it again. But I can't. I can only look back and realize that even if I had made a grave mistake by taking such a big gamble—and fell on my face—it would have worth it to leave the miserable job I'd had.

The only way to get a better life, man, job or whatever is to take that first step into the unknown. And, yes, this might cause some anxiety. When this happens, you know you've spent too much time in the comfort zone. You like your life. You like your job. And on and on and on. But don't you want to *love* your life and your job and, hopefully, a great man? Sure you do. But until you're ready, really, really ready, it probably won't happen.

The comfort zone is a place where a lot of us become stuck. We find ourselves in okay lives and that's *okay*. It's just *okay*. We don't want to rock the boat and we don't want to step on any toes. We have an okay life and we're lucky to have an okay life. We shouldn't be ungrateful. We might not want to incite any jealousy from others. We might not want to leave our comfortable existences, either. Sure, you've probably worked really hard to get where you are now. The thought of leaving it might be disconcerting. You have *this*, but you might have to give it up in order to get *that*. Sometimes people get afraid to get out of their routines because they don't have to think too much about anything.

Believe me, you're not giving anything up. Once you start flourishing, and you will, you'll wonder why you were anxious about all this in the first place. Mostly because it will be fun! Wouldn't it be wonderful to have a fun life? Yes, it would be! Wouldn't it be fantastic to finally date that man you've dreamed about? Absolutely! It should excite you to the point that you get up off your butt and do something. If it doesn't excite you, then you are definitely stuck in the comfort zone and gets stuck there can suck.

I want you to get excited about the new life you're envisioning for yourself. I want you to step over those anxieties about having what you want. I want you to overcome any self doubt you might have. And I want you to start right now. Think about how you want your life to be and instead of feeling a slight panic, feel an adrenaline rush. How? Just feel the excitement, that's how. Think of all the wonderful things you will do sometime soon. Once you feel that, you'll be well on your way to not only a better future, but a better *now*. And that's what it's all about.

What are you waiting for?

There comes a time when you have to be ready to take action. There comes a time when the same-old-same-old just isn't cutting it. So, the question is, "What are you waiting for?"

The best of us go through times of procrastination. It's just easier to let things slide. We're tired from work, our mothers are driving us up the wall and to actually take action to do something seems tiresome. That man we want looks good in theory, but we might think he's too much trouble to deal with right now. So, we set ourselves up to wait on him.

But, we only have a certain amount of time to do things on this earth and this means that the clock is always ticking. The time is now. Don't you think it's time to figure out what you really want? The problem with waiting to do anything is that you're always stuck waiting. Tomorrow or next week or even next year might seem like a good idea right now, but when those days come, it might be depressing to look back and see what you could have been doing then. Getting stuck is a human condition. Getting unstuck is a necessity. But many people never make the effort to get unstuck. Remember, time doesn't wait for anyone.

This is not to say you should panic and throw caution to the wind and do something crazy. All I am saying is there's no time like to present to sit down, figure out what you want and then go for it.

Once you can begin to understand all this and start to take action, you might realize that something else is stopping you. It might be procrastination, as mentioned above or it might be fear. Keep in mind that you have to be ready to do this. You have to be ready to make a change in your life. You have to be willing to take action, thereby, taking a chance. You have to be ready, ready, ready.

And if you're not ready? Then no book is going to help you attract anything into your life. This might mean you're stuck and, hey, we've all been there. If you are stuck and not ready to move forward, then put this book aside and come back to it later when you are ready to start manifesting your desires.

On this same note, many of us get into the loop of not wanting to wait for our desires to manifest. We want what we want—now! We're like Veruca Salt in *Charlie and the Chocolate Factory*—"Now, daddy!" And, yes, we can sometimes be as bratty as Veruca. This inability to wait, this impatience could be exactly what has kept you from getting what you want, whether it be a new man or a new car or more money.

"I don't want to wait until I'm old to enjoy my life." This is a phrase many of us use over and over. We might not say it out loud, but we think it. This phrase is edged with a little panic, with a little unease and it's a recipe for unhappiness. By always focusing on not waiting, we are actually putting ourselves in a spot *to* wait. Remember, the world delivers what you focus on and if all your focus is on waiting—guess what? That's all you'll be doing.

How do you turn it around? By not waiting! By starting to enjoy your life right now, today, this minute with or without the man of your dreams. If you take your focus off the wait, you'll probably be waiting a lot less. Impatience sometimes gets the best of us, but if you've been waiting for years on something or someone, this might be your problem. And it's so easy to correct! Like I said, all you have to do is start enjoying your life. All you have to do is stop waiting! By doing this, you will take the pressure off yourself and what you want will come to you. However, if you find yourself continuously waiting, then there's some reason why this is. Are you really just procrastinating or are you, perhaps, just too lazy to go after what you really want? Figure it out and then move on. And it doesn't hurt to ask yourself, "What exactly am I waiting on?"

Get over your fear of rejection.

Get over your fear of rejection. Rejection is tough. No one wants to be rejected in any way, shape or form. And yet, it still seems to happen from time to time. However, if you get hung up on rejection, you will never receive the gift of being wanted. And why is that? Because you begin to think of yourself as "lesser than." That's no way to be, either.

Fear of rejection is what stops most of us in our tracks. We're so afraid of getting rejected we won't attempt to do anything. We refuse to put ourselves out there for fear of more rejection. It's hard. I know it's hard. And what is the fear of rejection? Essentially, fear of rejection is fear of embarrassment. If you put yourself out there and you get rejected, that's humiliating, right? I know it is and I can speak from personal experience. Rejection is a bitch. I won't mince words. It's a bitch, a real, big and bad bitch.

The opposite of rejection is acceptance and acceptance is a basic human need. We need to feel accepted; in other words, we want to be wanted. Once we feel this, it builds confidence and allows us more freedom to expect better things in our lives. However, for some, getting this acceptance is hard. But you have to keep trying; you have to put yourself out there. And you have to keep doing this because somewhere, someone will finally accept you. Once that happens, more people will begin to accept you. And you will finally find the acceptance you've longed for.

But before that, why not just accept yourself? Why not embrace everything about yourself, faults and all? Of course, I would be lying if I said this was the same as others accepting us because it's not. But if we can just try to be more accepting of ourselves, maybe we can pave the way for others to begin to accept and want us.

Many of us get into this rejection/acceptance cycle because of our childhoods. Mom and dad might not have been so accepting. They may have been a little rejecting. This is very hard for any kid to deal with and when this happens, and the kid turns into an adult, the need to be accepted increases. But along with that need, we develop a fear of rejection and that fear of never being accepted for who we are can be disempowering.

So how do you get over your fear of rejection? You stop feeling rejected, that's how. I'm not saying you don't put yourself out there because, in a way, you will have to do that to a certain extent to be wanted. I mean, if the guys don't know you're alive, they can't hardly want you, can they? What I mean is this: Whenever something happens where you feel rejected, don't let it stop you. Keep going. Stop for one second and recognize how you feel—humiliated, let down, or whatever. Always recognize your feelings; just don't get hung up on them.

You might need to realize that if a person really likes themselves, it's harder for them to feel rejected because they're not trying so hard to get acceptance. Rather, they're just trying to make a connection. If they get rejected, it's no big deal because they realize that the person wasn't worth making a connection with. They see the situation for what it is—two people in a situation where they're not compatible—rather than through the narrow view of acceptance/rejection.

So, keep in mind that if you expect rejection, you will get it. Remember that you see what you most focus on and, if all your focus on is your fear of rejection that is exactly what you will get. Just turn it around by expecting acceptance! Tell yourself, "I will be liked by whomever I meet!" In time, once you really begin to believe that, you will. It's that simple. This is a great way to build your confidence, too. But what if you're still getting rejected? Keep trying. Soon enough, if you keep a good attitude, you'll find the acceptance you most desire.

Party girl central.

Before we move on, I want to touch on a few other things that might be keeping the man of your dreams from entering your life. The first is what I like to call the *party girl syndrome*. Sure, you party girls always have fun, but soon enough, you'll be the only one still partying. I am not saying to never go to a party or club. You should enjoy your life. But if it's interfering with getting a good man—and you know if it is or not—it's time to grow up.

If your goal is to get married and/or have children, you need to make this a priority and not waste too much time partying because the clock is ticking. I've seen older women do this and wonder why they don't have a husband and kids by now. They party too much! They're clubbing too much! They're hanging out with their friends too much. It will be hard for anyone to find a man when their social calendars are so full. Regardless, one day they wake up and realize that window of opportunity has closed.

We have to realize, as women, we only have a certain amount of time to procreate. Women in our generation have been told that it's okay to wait and for some, it is. For others, it means fertility treatments or other alternatives like adoption or surrogacy. I know this may sound a little heavy-handed for a dating book, and I don't mean to scare anyone with this bit of information, but I think it's a very important point to stress. I just think it's time we women wake up and realize we might have been given some wrong information when it comes to having kids. Of course, not all women want kids and that is fine—no judgments here! But if this is one of your priorities, you might want to keep this in mind. This does not mean to panic about it, either. This also doesn't mean that you should be desperate. It just means, keep this in mind if you're partying too much and not focusing on what you really want, which may or may not be kids.

So you have to prioritize. Maybe having a family isn't what you're exactly after right now. And that's okay. But you have to figure out what it is you want and then go after it. Time is a wasting and it's better to be safe than sorry.

Don't get hung up on the how.

One of my biggest assets is that I am a problem solver. It's also one of my biggest problems. I always get hung up on the how. *How are things going to work out? How do I do this? How, how, how?!*

Finally I figured out that I don't always know how! And guess what? You don't either. In other words, if you know what you want and you really want it badly enough, things will work themselves out for you to get it. This is the most important aspect of this book—knowing exactly what you want so you'll know it when you see it. This tends to get obscured when people get too hung up on the how.

Not knowing how things are going to turn out is fine. That means it might come as a surprise. The man of your dreams might just miraculously appear in your life overnight—hey, it could happen!—but he's going to get lost if you try to figure out *how* he's going to get there.

Of course, I am not saying a girl shouldn't try to do things and just wait for the arrival of Mr. Right on her doorstep. Rather, I'm saying, don't worry so much about how it's going to happen. Just stay open to new ideas and new things that life presents you. This is the way that things really happen for you. You just can't force it.

Sounds metaphysical and hippy-drippy, doesn't it? "Hey, man, let's let the universe take care of the how. We'll just sit back and wait for something to happen."

But that's essentially what you have to do. When it actually happens, then you can take appropriate action. And you will know when it's happening. But before that, let go of the outcome. Take the pressure off yourself to figure out how you're going to find this dreamboat. Don't worry about it.

But that's not so easy, is it? Well, if you change your perspective just a bit, it can be.

Have you ever gone on vacation and worried about how you're going to get there? Usually not. Usually you're thinking about your destination, right? Right. Sure, you might get stuck in some traffic or, perhaps, your flight might get delayed or cancelled, but you never let go of what you're doing—focusing on the destination. Soon enough, you're there, probably sipping a fruity tropical drink by the pool and enjoying yourself. "How" you got there never really entered your mind. You just always knew you would. And this is a great way to look at life.

By not focusing on how you're going to get there—to whatever want you most desire—you can actually start achieving what you want. "How" can become irrelevant! But getting hung up on the how is what most of us do. We focus so much on how we're going to do something we stop it from ever happening. This is nothing more than a control issue. We think that if something is completely and totally out of our control—which it kinda is—it won't ever happen. But if we prod it a little, or a lot, our desires will materalize that much more quickly. We have to realize that it doesn't matter how it will happen; it only matters that it will.

But if I don't worry about it, nothing will happen. Who says? Something will happen whether you're consciously involved or not. *But how am I going to do it?* Argh!

If you are in this line of thinking, you are definitely hung up on the how. But it's not your problem to solve. In fact, it's not a problem at all unless you make it one. It only matters *to you* and it is up *to you* to figure out what you want. This is the most important aspect of it—knowing what you want, so you'll know it when you see it. This gets obscured when people get hung up on the how. All you have to do is get the ball rolling.

It's called having faith. So, don't worry about the how, i.e. "How will I do it?" It will come to you via inspiration. And when it comes, you will know it beyond a shadow of a doubt.

Selfish much?

Ayn Rand wrote about the "virtue of selfishness". Was she onto something?

"But isn't this selfish of me? I mean, to get what I want out of life and to have all my desires fulfilled… Isn't it selfish of me to want to date a great man when others date total losers? Well, doesn't this make me something of an entitled bitch?"

No. Why do you think that? Well, it's just not you. It's a lot of us. We think that we can't have what we want because it's just too much to ask or expect. But mostly, we think we can't have it because, for some unknown reason, we don't deserve it. And it's not because we *don't* deserve it. This is just the way most of us have been brought up.

You have to get over this because this is just a recipe for misery. Selfish, to me, is a dangerous word because the fear of being perceived as selfish is what keeps us from going forward and keeps us going without what we want.

Until you get what you want out of life, you'll probably be miserable. If you're always dating losers or cheaters, you'll probably be miserable. Unless, of course, you're just a glutton for punishment. Dating good men who are considerate and make us laugh and who pay for dinner isn't just something selfish women do, it's something all women should do. In fact, we all deserve the better men. But, sometimes, the fear of looking selfish gets in the way of this.

Having what we want in life makes us happy. Dating good men can make you happy. I'm not saying you *have* to have money or the best looking guy to ever walk the earth to make you happy, but I'm saying it doesn't hurt. The problem is we feel as though we don't deserve these things, so we don't try. Also, we feel that if we suppress our real desires, we stave off disappointment. Not so. Once we push down our feelings and our desires, other things get pushed down too. Soon, you don't know why you're angry or when you're happy because you've denied yourself access to your own feelings. And it bleeds into other parts of your life.

Sometimes, people mistakenly let the idea of being selfish take over their personal lives in regards to what they want and to what they have. It's okay to share your abundance but it's not okay to keep yourself from getting more just so you can share in the misery. It's about not feeling guilty for wanting to succeed in whatever you do in life. Wanting to "do better" is not selfish.

Sure, it would be nice to bring along everyone when we succeed. We do want others to have success, right? Sure, we do. We want all of our friends to date good guys. Most of us have good intentions. However, it is up to each individual person to do this for herself. You can't give someone success, just as you can't "find" good men for your friends to date. It is their responsibility to do so. But you have to realize that just because they won't do this for themselves, doesn't mean you shouldn't do it for you.

But what can you do? Hold yourself back and not do what you want out of fear of being called selfish? Just don't try to date at all? Or can you go for the gusto and get what you want? This is not a slippery slope. This is either/or. And sometimes, you have to have the cajones to make the call.

You have to realize that if you are always serving this need to be viewed as selfless, you won't ever get anything you want in life. You will always end up empty-handed. And that will lead to martyrdom.

Let's use an analogy, which I like to call "The Last Piece of Cake." No one "wants" it because it might seem selfish to take it. Only if no one wants it will you dare take it. But you can't really have that last piece of cake without everyone looking at you like you're being selfish. And so, you do without.

"You're being awfully selfish," is nothing more than a form of manipulation so they can get you to do what they want. Forget what you want, it's about self-sacrifice! And don't eat that last piece of cake!

This sort of sacrifice comes from a fear of disappointing others, from a fear of *disapproval*. Oh, God, what if someone disapproves of us? How would we ever be able to take it?

A lot of this stems from the fact that most girls are raised to seek approval before they do anything. No, it isn't fair, but recognizing it for what it is—basic manipulation—can take a great weight off your shoulders. *Huh, so it's not bad of me to want more out of life?* No, it's really not!

Of course, I am not saying to go and plow though others to get what you want. I am not saying to neglect your kids, if you have them. I am not saying to impose on others and force them to do what you want. That's not what the Law of Attraction is about. It's about knowing what you want and attracting it to you. It's not about waiting around until every else is comfy and ready for you to move forward. And your fear of being called selfish could be just what's keeping you from getting what you really want out of life.

Just think about it. Why is getting what you want out of life considered selfish? At least you're taking care of someone! But, it's self-serving, isn't it? So? Does it mean we have no consideration for others? No. It just means you can have your cake and eat it to. Go for it.

Yes, you can.

We all have read the book *The Little Engine That Could* by Watty Piper. It's a classic children's book with a really good message. That message is, when all the other trains couldn't or wouldn't do something, the little train that could came along and did it. She wasn't the biggest or best train in the world but she tried. And by trying she succeeded: "I think I can, I think I can, I think I can."

But sometimes before you get to the point of thinking you can do something, doubt has to rear its ugly head. This happens to the best of us. We're going along, going after what we want when, all of a sudden, we think, "Oh, no, what if I can't do this? What if I *shouldn't* do it?" Remember what I said about the "what if-ing"? It's just fear. And some say that fear is simply "false evidence appearing real". So, whenever you find yourself doubting, cover that thought with a powerful intention. When you think, "I don't think I can do this," replace it with, "I think I can do it. I just need to have faith that I can." And then, "I can do this! I will do this!"

And ta da! You're in business! You are the little lady that could and that little lady that could will become the little lady that does.

Going, going, gone.

I think one of the main problems people have when using the Law of Attraction has to do with one simple word. And that word? *Going to.* Actually, that's two words. Even so, these two little words have kept a lot of people from getting what they want out of life.

Going to.

Look at those two words for a good long second. *Going to.* Think about them. What do they mean? They mean that someday you're *going to* do something. *Going to.*

Never gonna happen. Or at least it's less likely to. And why is this? If you're going to do something that means sometime in the future you will do something. That means it won't happen because the future is always *in* the future and by the time you get there, you'll probably forget about your intentions or just give up on them. This is also like saying, "I'll get around to it one of these days." However, "one" of these days never comes and you never get around to it. It's just another way of procrastinating about what you want.

Let's use some examples:
- "I am going to lose weight."
- "I am going to get a good man."
- "I am going to have the life I want."
- "I am going to go on vacation someday soon."

The problem with "going to" is this: It's always in the future! It's never in the now. Going to is a good intention but if you're going to do something, you'll never do it.

Do you get it?

And all you have to do is change those two little words around and set your intention in stone. And so "going to" becomes "I will."

Here are some examples:
- "I will lose this weight."
- "I will get a good man."
- "I will have the life I most desire."
- "I will go on vacation."

Now you're talking!

There you go. Of course, as I've said and will say throughout the book, once you put what you intend to do out there, when the opportunity arises, you have to act. Without action, nothing will happen in your life.

You must put yourself out there.

You must put yourself out there. Why? Because if the men don't know you're alive, they can't hardly want you, can they?

Once you integrate all of this into your life, men will start coming out of the woodwork. In addition to this, you will get a few ideas of your own about how to start dating a better class of men. (This is where inspiration will take place, right after you state your intention and it usually comes in the form of ideas that just pop into your head.) However, the more you put yourself in a situation where you can meet better men, do so.

Additionally, I think there are things a girl can do to put herself out there more. There are professional matchmakers who work wonders. Some of them only charge the men. It's their job to match you with the right person. And, as an added bonus, the men who employ professional matchmakers are serious about meeting someone and usually serious about settling down. And we all know that like attracts like, right? Therefore, if this is your goal, too, this might be an avenue to look into.

Also, online dating has lots of benefits. However, the downside is that you might have to meet a few frogs before you find your prince.

But I think the best place to find men is anywhere. That's right. Men are everywhere you are. And the great thing is a lot of them are available and looking, just like you!

The possibilities are endless! Just think about it. And smile. You're getting ready to come into your own.

Once you've begun your journey to dating a good man and getting a better life, you might stop every once in a while and think, *Is this really working?*

You will know if it's working or not. If you're not sure, keep in mind that it might not come in the form you think. It might come through an invite to lunch, or a chance encounter at a bookstore or whatever. It might come from a job opening in another city, even though you had never considered relocating. It might come from a last minute vacation invite by a friend who just happens to have an extra ticket to some tropical location or to a cruise. It doesn't matter where it comes from; all that matters is that it does. What's important is being open to all possibilities and not closing yourself off to any new prospects. You could meet someone when you're walking your dog!

With this frame of mind, never turn down an invite. If someone asks you to lunch on your job, go. If someone mentions that everyone is meeting for drinks after work and you're invited—go! If someone invites you to a family barbeque—go! Or fireworks show or whatever, just go! Go! Go! Go!

And why? Because the more you are out and about, the greater your chances for meeting men. And that's what we're after, people! Soon enough, you won't wonder if it's working. You'll know it is.

Keep in mind that if you're out in the world, you are going to see a lot of men. And that means, when you feel wanted you will automatically attract them to you.

Out of focus.

Think about your life right now. How focused are you on getting what you want out of life? How committed are you to doing what you want to do? How badly do you want the best relationship of your life? Are you focused on what you want or what you have to do?

"But, but, I have so many other things to worry about right now. I have bills to pay and I have to walk the dog and my mom called and work is crazy and right now I don't think I can fit a new man into my life. But soon, soon, I swear I will work on all this and then I'll be happy. But right now, I am so scattered and I just hate it, but that's just the way life is, right?"

Wrong.

Read that paragraph over again. Does it sound familiar to you? What is it saying? It's saying you're so scattered that none of your attention is on anything you want. It's all on doing stuff you *have* to do. It's not necessarily about don't-wants, but have-tos. *You have to do so and so. There's no time for yourself.* That paragraph is about a pretty hard life that isn't so much about fun. And what is it focused on? Your lack of control over your own life!

You might be so focused on what you have to do you're completely unfocused on what you want to do! And this brings us to my point: Life can be hectic, but once you only focus on what you don't really want—a hard life—that's probably all you'll get. And how can a new man ever enter into this without him adding to the "have-tos"? He can't! Sure, you can start seeing him, but all you might be doing is adding him to the long list of your "to-dos". "Oh, I forgot to call Dan. I guess I'll have to find time to somehow squeeze him in.

No. No. No.

If this is your life right now, it might just be what's keeping you from having a good relationship with a good man. And all of this brings me to my point... Ready? Sit tight and listen. And learn. And now for one of the single most important aspects to the Law of Attraction and, I believe, life...and here it is: *What you focus on is what you get.*

It's that simple. Say, for instance, you feel a little apprehensive about flying somewhere. All of your attention is on that flight, the fear of being out of control, a fear of the turbulence. No matter what you do, you can't get the image out of your mind. By the time you arrive at the gate, you're panicking, thinking you can't get on the plane, that you're going to freak out. But you do get on the plane. You don't freak out. There isn't much turbulence and you arrive at your destination in one piece and happy you went through with it.

But why were you worried in the first place? You took one little fear and turned it into a great big monster. You focused too much on your fear of flying and not enough about your destination! You weren't thinking about the tropical paradise you were flying to, you were thinking about something "bad" happening. The same applies to your life. If all you focus on is what you have to do, what you want gets pushed aside.

It's all about focus, it really and truly is. What you focus on is what you get. If you keep your focus on everything bad in your life and how hard your life is right now—guess what—you're going to get more bad and your life will be become that much harder. It's that simple. So, what can you do? Change your focus and this will change your life. Change your focus and then change your ideas about dating. Change your ideas about dating and start living—actually living!—the life you want, with the man of your choosing. How great is that?

Being so out of focus about what you want might actually keep your desires from appearing. This is why it's so important to know what you want and to focus on that and not all this other stuff which won't matter a year from now. However, if you start to focus on what you want, a year from now you could have it all! It's really that simple!

So, change your focus, change your life and start living today! All those things you have to get done can be done sometime. But it's important to start focusing on what you want. Once you start prioritizing and place the stuff that you want to do a little higher on your list, you will actually start getting what you want out of life.

Giving up on him.

Most women have this one guy they long for. And lust after. He's "The One.". He's perfect in every way, shape and form. He's the *man I want*. As you're reading all this, some doubt might creep into your mind and you might begin to wonder: "But what if I don't ever get him?"

He may be the man you've wanted for ages. He may be some guy you see occasionally at the coffee shop. You've probably been so focused on him, you've kept a lot of other good men out of your life.

Who? Me? Keeping other men out of my life? Never!

Hold on there a minute, girlfriend. Come on. This may just be your problem. You see, in order to be wanted, you kinda, sorta need to be *available* to be wanted. And if you're hung up on the guy at the coffee shop or who sits in the cubical across from you, you're not attracting anything into your life. Except the sound of crickets.

It's true. You're probably blocking all these other dudes from stepping into your life and rocking your world. So, what can you do? You give up on him. Obviously, if it was going to happen with this guy, it would have happened already. But, of course, that's not to say it won't happen. And I'd be willing to be that once you let this one go and you start getting what you want out of life, he'll jump on the bandwagon. They always do. They never see you for you until you become attractive to someone else. And unless you unblock yourself with this one guy, you're not available to become attractive to anyone else.

Let me put it a bit differently. Have you ever been with a guy you just absolutely loved? Remember how you just didn't see other guys, how you just didn't notice them? Well, that's what you're doing now—but you're single! Therefore, you're blocking all these other guys from having a chance at you. And, let's be honest, there might just be someone else out there who would be better for you in the end other than this one guy.

The problem with this obsession over this one guy is this: You think that if you get him, you'll finally be okay. Right? Let me tell you something, you are okay with or without him and once you start believing that, you *will be* okay. Embrace your life now—without him. And get a move on. You've got men to torture.

Still not convinced? Surely, you're not that obsessed over this one guy. But maybe you are. Maybe you're saying to yourself, "*Wait a minute, you're telling me to do vision boards and manifest my desires to put all this effort out just to give up on the one guy I want?*"

Yes, I am. And I'll tell you why.

You're fixated on this guy. You want him for your boyfriend or husband. Maybe you want him to father your children. This guy could be someone you've known awhile or just met or just see occasionally in the subway. But he has everything you want and that's why you're fixated.

Well, don't be. Don't ever get too fixated on any one man—at least not until after you have him. For all you know, this guy isn't the one. He could be and if he is, it will happen. However, if he's not, then it's someone else, someone, perhaps, you haven't met yet.

Remember what I said about giving up on the "how"? This is part of it. You have to give up on how it's going to happen because you don't control that. All you have to do is have faith that it will happen someday soon.

But what about the Law of Attraction? Isn't this supposed to work for whatever man I want? Not necessarily. You will get the man you want, but he might not be the man you think he is, meaning, the man you're obsessed with now might not be the one you eventually end up falling for. It might be some other dude.

So, release him. Let him go. Give up on the "how". Give up on him. And sit back and wait. Now allow whatever is going to happen to happen. And then, receive.

You have to realize that one of the problems we have with all of this is that we want to control everything. Well, surprisingly enough, we're not in control, no matter how badly we want to be. So, when you free yourself by giving up on the "how" and on "the one", you open yourself up to many more possibilities. This means you shouldn't wait at home for him to knock on your door, but continue to put yourself out there so he can, perhaps, find you. How's that for a great concept? He might just be looking for you. Think about it. That's pretty sweet. One more note on this subject. Sometimes, when we want a certain man, he might already belong to someone else. So, it's imperative that you never break up any existing relationship—let them crumble on their own. Even if you think the relationship is on its last legs, even if he tells you he's out the door. (Bear in mind he might be lying.) This is bad Karma and remember: If they'll do it *with* you, they will do it *to* you.

To reiterate: Don't get hung up on one man. That's getting hung up on the "how" and if you want the Law of Attraction to work in your favor, you should know by now that's one thing you shouldn't do.

Just desserts.

Have you ever had a really good dessert and thought, "I want some more of that!" *That's* the Law of Attraction in action.

Once you get the Law of Attraction and really start to attract the things and relationships you want in life, you will automatically begin to attract more. This is because you are living a life of joy and you are bringing more joy to yourself. So, whenever something really good happens in your life, say to yourself, "I want more of that!" And then accept it when it happens.

It's really that easy. And it will be even more delicious than the best dessert you've ever eaten when it happens to you.

Embrace your life. *Now.*

One thing that might be keeping everything you want from coming into your life is your inability—or refusal—to embrace what you have now. By that I mean, until we recognize all the good things in our lives and show appreciation for them, new good things might not come. You have to show gratitude. By doing this, you have to appreciate what you have now and this allows more good things to come into your life. In effect: *You embrace it now because it's good.* If you disown it, it will be hard for any new good thing to enter in.

Sometimes, though, it's hard. It's hard to show gratitude for a job you hate or a bad dating streak. It's hard to be pleased at all the terrible men you may have dated in the past. However, this is a form of resistance and once you resist what you have, you are putting a wall up between yourself and what you want. And that's no way to live.

The things in your life that you are not so pleased with might be keeping your intentions from happening. Many of us get into this funk and there we stay, wondering why life can't be just a little bit better, a little bit easier. Procrastination takes over and in some ways, we give up. We look at things we have in our lives and want better, thinking what we have now is worthless. And, therefore, this mindset keeps us from actually getting better. The point is, by not showing any appreciation for what you have, you put yourself in a position where you *can't* change. No, you *can* change but only when the circumstance is perfect can you move forward. Until then, you will wait. But how long are you willing to wait?

Remember, you can get what you want. It might not be in the exact form you envisioned, but it will come. With men, most of them won't be exactly what you are looking for so you may stop yourself from giving them a chance. They might be too this or too that, so you might let that opportunity slip by you. And then it'll slip again and again. All because of your so-called exacting standards. All because of your inability to open your eyes to what can be instead of focusing on what isn't.

But it's never too late. It's never too late to change! You could start today and in a year have your whole life turned around, if you would just start. But if you're waiting for something better to come along in order to be happy... Well, guess what? Something better might not come and it might not come because you're failing to recognize the rut you're in.

This could happen to the best of us. As we wait on our something better, our lives start to suck and that's because we're not appreciating what we have now. We're not recognizing we do have some good stuff now. We're just waiting for the better stuff to come along and make us happy. The problem is, even if it did show up, our perspective is so warped, we might not even be aware of it.

However, we get fearful of settling. If we settle for this old house, a newer, bigger one will never come along. If we settle for this old job, one with higher pay and better benefits won't come along. We think by settling that we're blocking better things from coming into our lives but the exact opposite is true! By not settling and by not appreciating what we have now, we're blocking better! I'm not saying to date any old man that comes along. But I am saying, why not at least give some of them a chance? You can go out on a few dates with men you wouldn't normally like and might find there are things you *do* like about some of them. This doesn't mean you have to marry any of them, but it will show you what you do and don't want. By blocking off anything new from coming into your life, you are setting yourself up for major unhappiness.

This leads to enormous amounts of discontentment. When you do this, you are focused on what you don't have. Remember what I said about focus? If all your focus is entirely on your future wants, nothing will ever be good enough *now*.

Contentment does not mean stagnation. It does not mean we're going to be stuck. Embrace what you have while you wait for your desires to happen. This is an important step in the Law of Attraction—you must appreciate what you have now. So, before you can get something new in your life, appreciate all your old stuff.

I think we have a fear of embracing what we have. We believe it will block anything new from coming in. No. No. And no. This is wrong. Go ahead and do a few projects around your place. Fix it up a little. "But I don't want to stay here," you say. Ah ha! Get it? You should. *You don't want to stay there.* And if you focus on what you don't want, guess what? That's what you'll get.

Honor and love everything in your life. Stop right now and honor whatever you have in your life. Seriously. Stop right now and think about what you have an embrace it. Maybe you have a cute dog or a nice apartment. Maybe you don't. Regardless, stop and honor the good things in your life.

You might be stumped. *What does she mean?* I mean, pay gratitude. You might not realize it, but before you can bring your true wants and desires into your life, you must first be grateful for what you have.

I have this belief that it's almost impossible to move forward if you don't first appreciate what you have. For example, every place I've ever lived in, I've honored when I was there. And I honored each place by fixing them up, decorating and cleaning. Granted, when I was younger, I lived in some dumps, so this was also a necessity. Regardless, whenever I'd move into a new place, I'd get to work fixing it up. And each new place was always better than the last. And I believe this is because I never took any place I lived for granted.

The same thing with my cars. Each car I've had has gotten better. I don't mean to come off as materialistic, because I'm not, but I am trying to make a point here. Until you honor and love and embrace what you have—no matter how crappy you might think it is—it's going to be almost impossible to get better.

Don't take anything for granted. By honoring what you have, by embracing your life now, you are showing gratitude. Remember, like attracts like and one of the easiest ways to get what you want is to start appreciating what you have.

The highlight analogy.

If you're still unsure of how all this works and how you can apply it to your life, let me use what I like to call the "highlight analogy".

Say you want highlights in your hair but they're too expensive or you don't have the time or can't find the right hair stylist or whatever. So you think you'll never get them. But you want them, really badly. The "how" of getting them hasn't worked itself out just yet.

Boom—this is your intention, to get highlights. This is what you want. But until you really feel like this is something you can do and believe in it, it won't happen until you make the decision to go for it. So, you decide you're going to do it—sometime. Slowly, very slowly, you begin to see the possibility in getting your highlights. And then you forget about it. You release the desire. Sure, it's still in the back of your mind and you occasionally think about it, but you don't really *do* anything about it.

So, you have your intention to get highlights and you begin to believe this is a possibility. One day you're walking by a salon that isn't busy and they have a sign out front for highlights and it's something you can afford. And you have the day off, so you can get what you want. This is your day! Of course, it might not be the salon you would have preferred to go to or whatever, but this is what you wanted, being manifested for you.

But until you put it into action—actually entering the salon and asking for highlights—it won't happen. Your desire is manifested right here, but if you decide this isn't exactly what you wanted, and don't go for it, then you won't get it.

I think it's rare that a desire is the exact thing we wanted. I mean, it is, but it usually doesn't come in the nice little package we would have liked. So, by using this analogy, you can apply it to any situation, especially dating. Say you want a man, but you want a *certain* kind of man. A new man enters your life but he's not exactly your type, but he's got some other great attributes. You really dig him, but you think you might want to hold out and wait for someone better. So, you let this opportunity pass you by. And then another one comes into your life, but it's the same story—not exactly what you wanted. Soon enough, you've given up hope of ever meeting *anyone* when, all along, you were meeting great men, but you just couldn't see it. And then frustration and anger sets in and by then, you've given up.

I think this might be called "not seeing the forest for the trees". When you want something, you have to be ready to take it when it comes your way. But if you keep passing it up, waiting for something else you think you might want more, then you'll never get anything you want.

Sure, most of us get into the mindset of not wanting to settle. But who says you're settling if the exact, perfect man doesn't come along? Who says you're settling if you get offered a great job but it doesn't have the exact, perfect pay and benefits you were looking for? Once you begin to accept what the world offers, then you will see that other areas open up in your life. The men will begin to work out once you let them.

So, I say, open up to the possibilities! Take a chance! Get your hair done and then let it down! Once you free yourself of preconceived notions of how things "should" be, then you will see the wonder of how things can work out by simply letting go of what you thought *should* be and getting onto what *can* be.

Coming from a position of lack.

Many of us, whether we realize it or not, are coming from a position of lack. What this means is that we're fixated on what we "don't" have, and we don't ever stop to appreciate what we do have. Once we have this belief instilled in us—and it could be a subconscious belief we're not even aware of—we continue on a path of not having what we want. When you come from this position of lack, you kind of give up on things. But if you're positive, you remain open to things happening.

However, getting there might be a problem. Once we're on this path of lack, "lack" is pretty much all we're going to have. From wardrobes to men to money, it's all the same. "Lack" overtakes our lives and we feel as though we're not good enough for anything.

But how do we get to this point? Because that's what we're feeling. If we think we don't have this or that, then we won't ever have it. For instance, if you've never had a good boyfriend in the past, you might be coming from a position of lack and think that because you've never *had* one, you'll never *have* one.

Say you want a new sofa, for instance. You've found the one you want from some fancy store where they cost into the thousands. But it is the one you *want*. You've perused the catalogues, the internet and even the store looking at this one sofa. But, you can't afford it, right?

One day, you're invited over to an acquaintance's house for some cocktails. And guess what? They have your sofa! And, boy, does it make you mad. You think, "How can they afford that sofa and I can't? It's not fair!"

This is coming from a position of lack. If you believed that one day the sofa was going to be yours, you'd sit down on it, admire it, ask your hostess where she got it and how much she spent, if you had the nerve. You would think to yourself, "One day, I will have that sofa." And once you get that attitude, I'll almost guarantee you that one day you will have it. You might win some money on a scratch-off to get it. It might be on clearance. Someone might have a used one in good shape that they're selling for nothing. (And this can happen, as I once saw a leather Chesterfield couch on the internet for two-hundred bucks, which was so cheap, it made my head spin.)

So, whenever you find yourself feeling lacking, stop and say, "I will have what I want. I don't know how, but I will." This is a good change in perspective and can work wonders in your dating life. Just by recognizing that you're doing this, you can set yourself up for better dating experiences from here on out.

And there you go. You're on your way to a much better existence and soon you will be coming from a position of abundance.

Mr. Right and the evil he causes.

Mr. Right, in theory, sounds so good. He's a good looking guy with a great sense of humor. He's smart, comes from a good family and has great taste in jewelry. Oh, if only every girl could have her very own Mr. Right.

Unfortunately, none of us can have him. And why is that? Because he doesn't exist, that's why. And because he's just a fantasy most women create in their minds, he tends to cause a lot of unrealistic expectations and, inevitably a lot of disappointment. Therefore, he's kinda evil.

One of the greatest disservices women do to themselves is to look for Mr. Right and then to hold out for Mr. Right. They pass lots of good men up because they have their mind set on this one perfect man. He's so this and he's so that and he's just so perfect, you can't stand it. He's just the best. However, he doesn't exist. Men are human and are not perfect. Therefore, Mr. Right doesn't exist.

However, once you latch onto the idea of the perfect man, Mr. Right, no other man will do. Other men, simply, won't measure up. We all want the man who will be best for us, but many women delve off into fantasy land too much. They come up with this image of a man who is just out of this world. A guy that no human could possibly measure up to!

So, my advice is to get Mr. Right out of your head. He doesn't exist and if you have an image of this perfect man in your mind, no man will ever live up to those expectations. In the end, you will only wind up disappointment.

One reason we get so hung up on Mr. Right is because we want someone to watch over us. We go into relationships, and even jobs, thinking that this person or company will take care of us. This engenders a false sense of security. Here's a better idea: Take care of yourself!

It's good, nice even, to rely on others, but you need to be able to stand securely on your own two feet. And you can do it. You can take care of yourself. All you have to do is have faith in your ability to make it on your own. Knowing you can get through today and tomorrow is all you need to do. Sure, the bills may be piling up or whatever, but by fantasizing about someone—Mr. Right, perhaps?—swooping in and taking care of you will give you nothing but insecurity. It's nice to fantasize but by always holding out, you're doing nothing but letting life pass you by.

Out of the belief that comes with the idea that someone will take care of us, comes the realization that we *should* take care of ourselves and that we should start today. Once you decide to begin to love a better life, it might be a good idea to take stock of where you are now in regards to finances, etc. The best thing you can do is take care of all this extraneous stuff, which will free your mind and allow the joy to start taking place.

In essence, instead of waiting on Mr. Right, get your act together now. Even if Mr. Right did show up to "fix" everything, if your personal life is a mess, nothing he can do will enable you to move forward. That's why it's so important to start today.

So, forget Mr. Right. Forget about someone taking care of you for the rest of your life. And start taking care of yourself. As soon as you do this, *your* Mr. Right, with all his imperfections, will come along and you can begin to build a good life together with him. Remember, none of us are perfect, so how can we expect the man we want to be perfect? That's just unrealistic.

The problem of unrequited love.

You love him. He doesn't love you. He loves someone else—or, worse, himself—more. This puts a want, a desire in you mind. You have to have him. Soon, he becomes an obsession. Before you know it, you're googling him or, worse, hanging out at places you know he might be. Soon, you feel like crap about yourself but there's nothing you can do, right? You're in love with someone who doesn't love you. You are experiencing unrequited love.

I hate to say it, but it must suck to be you. Finding yourself in this position will not only make a fool out of you, it will keep a lot of good stuff from happening in your life. In essence, unrequited love blocks real love from entering your life.

So, what can you do? You can give up on this guy. You can release him. You can move on. It might be hard, but it's what you have to do in order to get on with your life.

However, unrequited love can sometimes work in your favor. And that's basically what you're doing when you don't let the man you most desire know how much you want him. This will drive him crazy over you. He will get into that position of thinking you're holding out on him and it will make him want you even more. And, when you get him, and you will know when you've gotten him, then you can give that love back.

Not a bad trade-off. Let him do all the work and you get the reward. And isn't this how it's supposed to be? Men used to have to work for women. They wouldn't get a woman if they didn't. Now, they think all they have to do is show up. And God forbid if they have to buy flowers or pay for dinner! This mindset men have nowadays is just wrong. Women *should* be taken care of by men in this way—it's just basic consideration, after all. However, if you allow him to walk all over you, you'll just end up alone anyway.

So, this is your goal when dealing with men. You want to make him want you more than you want him. It has to be this way; otherwise you will always be in the receiving end of unrequited love.

In any relationship, the desire is rarely equal. One always wants the other more than the other wants the one. There is a "wanted" and a "wantee". You have to put yourself in the position of being the "wantee". And it's really not that hard once you learn how to do it.

Guilt and validation.

Get over your guilt. It's that simple. *Get over your guilt.* Guilt is one way we block ourselves from living fulfilled lives and getting the men we most want. Guilt blocks us from lots of things, including happiness. But what, exactly, is this thing called guilt?

Guilt is something we feel when we think we've done something wrong. Subsequently, we make ourselves pay for it by feeling terrible. So, figure out what you feel guilty about—a past relationship, slacking on the job, whatever—and ask yourself if you've paid enough. If so, get over it.

Guilt does nothing but make us feel bad. Sure, it might keep us on track and on the straight and narrow, but mostly it just clings to us in ways that come out in everything we do. If we feel guilty because we haven't called our mothers, that might come out in feeling bad about eating a brownie. Soon enough, guilt will take over our lives and we won't know what we're feeling or when. And that's because guilt is overshadowing everything we do. Suddenly, we're bad all the way through, just because we might have fibbed a little on our time at work or "forgot" to call our best friend or whatever.

The way I see it, stuff happens every single day. We can't control that. But we start thinking we can by feeling bad about things that don't deserve our attention.

One way to get over guilt once and for all is to stop seeking validation. By this I mean, stop looking for someone else to approve of what you do. Sure, you could do things better sometimes, but sometimes you just can't. Sometimes it's hard to do the right thing.

Say, for instance, you have a puppy and your landlord tells you to get rid of him. Try as you may, no one wants the dog. You're stuck with him but you can't be stuck with him or you're going to invalidate your lease agreement and be out on the street. You start to feel guilt every time you look at the puppy, but what can you do? You ask over and over to everyone you talk to, "What can I do now?" Well, no one knows what you can do with the puppy and no one really cares. You wait and you wait, thinking something might happen, someone might come along and take the puppy, but inevitably, you have to take him to the pound.

A horrible scenario, I know.

So, you take him to the pound and feel horrible about it. You talk about it incessantly to everyone, trying to get someone to tell you that you did the right thing. And no one will. No one will validate what you did. They all say you shouldn't have been stupid and got the puppy in the first place, that you should have known better. So, what happens now? Guilt steps in and soon enough, you're having anxiety about the puppy and about what an awful person you are.

See how it works? One little thing suddenly becomes a mountain to which you must climb. Sometimes climbing that mountain is impossible. I say stop when you get tired. I say, stop when you can't take it anymore. I say, don't even go there. I say, sometimes it is hard to always be perfect. And, lastly, I say, other people don't know what you have been through and, therefore, have no business passing judgment.

What all this means in the end is that you're not perfect. Hey, join the human race! None of us are perfect! And guess what? You never have been and you never will be and that fact is what makes each and every one of us unique. But until you get over seeking validation, which leads to guilt, you will have a hard time putting yourself out there to be wanted. And that's just taking up precious space in your mind that could be put to better use, as in attracting the things you really want in your life that make you happy and make you feel like a worthwhile person. And a worthwhile person rarely, if ever, feels guilt. So, neither should you.

Also guilt can make you think that you're undeserving. Why do you deserve this? Why do you deserve to feel wanted? This is where you're failing. You don't think you deserve it. Get this idea out of your head. Of course you deserve whatever you want in life. Why shouldn't you?

And get over your guilt. Sure, we all make mistakes and must atone but that doesn't mean you have to sentence yourself to a lifetime of feeling miserable.

Find your joy. Follow your bliss.

A fresh bouquet of flowers. A new silk nightgown. A really great bra. These little things help you experience joy and joy is what you need to feel so you can begin to experience a good life.

Remember when I talked about coming from a position of lack? Well, when we never do nice things for ourselves, we are saying we're not worth it. This is basically "doing without." Yes, times may be tough, money may be tight, but if you never give yourself anything in life you really want and enjoy, you will live a miserable existence. I am not saying to go out and break the bank. I'm not saying to put a new pair of shoes on your credit card. I'm saying, we can all find a little money here or there to give us something we will enjoy.

Figure out what you'd like and really want it. Start with something small, maybe a charm for a charm bracelet you one day hope to own. If you want it badly enough, you will find a way to get it.

You see, the little joys you experience will inevitably lead to bigger joys. Once you start experiencing joy, more will come along and that's because you begin to bring more joy to yourself. In this case, more equals more. However, our lives are so packed full of chaos, it's hard to experience any joy. But it's so important to find a way and start today. Even if it's just buying a pack of bubble gum you used to chew as a kid and loved, do it. Experience that bubble gum joy again.

When everything is all work and no play... Well, we all know how that always turns out. So, have some fun! Take some time to relax and enjoy life. Find your joy and follow your bliss. By doing this, you are creating the life you want to live. Start today to get the life you want. And once today gets good, tomorrow will be even better.

The secrets of self confidence.

Without confidence, you have nothing.

Confidence is being willing to take a risk by believing in yourself. Some of us have a fear of being confident because we secretly believe it draws attention to ourselves, thus setting us up for a good dressing down by others. *If they don't notice me, they won't hurt me.* So untrue. But we get afraid, don't we? We get afraid to be too overconfident. If you keep it to yourself, it's confidence. If you don't hide it, it's arrogance. There is a fine line here and all you have to do is be confident and let it show, but don't brag.

However, if we want to be wanted and desired by men, we have to have confidence. There's no way around it. Sure, you can be the wallflower, if you so choose, but you'll be the last girl asked to dance, if at all. It might be a harsh reality, but if you can't take it upon yourself to have a little confidence and get out there and get what you want, you will always be the wallflower. Sorry, the truth hurts but that's just the way it is.

The good news is you don't have to be the wallflower. You can be the showstopper! And all you have to do is become confident. And how do you do that? It's easy. All you have to do is act as if you *are* who you want to be. You know the old adage, "Fake it until you make it"? Use that to build your confidence. Act as if you are already the person you want to be. And you know what? You are that person already! All you're doing is bringing her forth.

Use this self confidence to get what you want out of life. In effect, state your intention as though it has already happened. It's easy: "I am dating a good man." There! Keep saying that to yourself and soon you will be! Say something else: "I am a great person!" And believe it! Act as if you are! And so you will be! Having confidence means committing yourself to the process and following through. Having confidence means you can do anything you set your mind to. You know you will do it because you're confident. It works, every time!

Act as though you are one day going to get what you want. Believe it's yours. Remember, "Fake it until you make it"? Well, do that. *Fake it until you make it.* This builds confidence and gives you hope for the future.

If you are self confident enough, you can admit you're wrong on some things—it's okay. Overall, you're still okay. It doesn't make you any less of a person. However if you lack confidence, admitting a mistake is like pulling teeth. You just can't do it, you just can't be wrong.

If you lack confidence, you know you will never get what you want. Right? You just *know* it. That's lack of confidence! That's all it is! You can have what you want and one of the keys steps in attaining it is confidence. And yet, it's hard to get that confidence. If it grew on trees, we'd all have it, right? Well, it doesn't have to grow on trees for you to get it. All you have to do is start believing in yourself.

As I said earlier, some women have a fear of standing out. Again, that's lack of confidence. *If people see me, they might do something to me.* But what could they do really? Make fun of you? So what? Bob Dylan once said, "If you haven't been booed, you haven't done anything." Isn't that true? Without trying, you can never hope to win. You have to keep in mind that sometimes you will win and sometimes you will lose. That's life. That's the same deal with men, too.

Some men you will automatically win over and some you won't.

Forget failure. You can only fail if you stop trying. So, don't stop trying! Also, stop worrying about perfection. No one is perfect and if that's what you're concerned about, you're not really living.

Lack of confidence can bleed over into almost all areas of your life. It can be seen in people who just can't make a decision. They don't have the confidence to commit to anything. As a result, they become stuck.

If you want more self confidence, you can do all the things I've discussed here. What could it hurt? It won't make you feel any worse about yourself, will it? In addition to that, another good way to build self confidence is to educate yourself. Become interesting by going out and doing something. It doesn't matter what, just do something. Go to a bookstore or a library or a museum. If you don't have a variety of subjects in your mind to draw from, your pool of men will greatly decrease.

In the end, confidence is key. It's just so important. Learning to have more confidence should be on any woman's agenda. You don't have to be arrogant, you don't have to brag, but you do have to know that you are good enough. Once you know that, you can do anything. And guess what? You are good enough! You're good enough to do anything you want! If no one else will tell you, or you won't tell yourself, I'll tell you—you're good enough! Live with it! You can do just about anything you set your mind to! All you have to do is go for it.

Jealousy and how it can help you get what you want.

Lack of confidence goes along with that old green-eyed monster, jealousy. Jealousy is a complex emotion born out of insecurity. Because it breeds insecurity, jealousy can be what some would call a "bad" emotion. However, you can take this emotion and use it to your advantage. How? Think of a person you've always been a little envious of and, yes, we all have one. She may be prettier, taller, smarter or whatever more than you. So what? Emulate her.

You say, "But I can't stand her!" But why can't you stand her? Think about it.

Some say we are jealous of others because they have similar traits to us. I have always thought this was a bunch of nonsense. If they were like us, wouldn't we like them *more*? We'd have a lot in common! Maybe we're jealous of others simply because we're jealous of something they have that we think we don't. This is true, to a certain extent. But I think it really boils down to is this: I think we're jealous of others who have what we have but know how to work it better than us. *That's* what we're really jealous of.

But guess what? None of us are lacking! You, too, can be as smart, pretty and as nice as this chick. Of course, if you're shorter than her, that could be a problem. But you get my point.

The great thing about the Law of Attraction is that once you start to use it, you will finally figure out you *can* get what you want out of life. It's thinking that you can't do what you want that leads to the negative thinking and jealousy is sometimes just a by-product of that. Jealousy can be overridden once you get confidence and getting what you want out of life can give you loads of confidence. Anything in life can be overridden once you get confidence. As you read this, you might think to yourself, "That's not for me, that's for other girls." This doesn't just cover dating, but other life situations, too. You deserve what other girls have. You already have it. You just have to bring it out.

The art of the conversation.

Many women get intimidated when they are faced with what is commonly known as "the conversation". This happens sometime on the first date when all the little chit-chat has dried up and the conversation begins to lull. You think, "Huh, now what?" That's a tough one. But, if you want to be wanted, you might need to be a good conversationalist.

Being a good conversationalist is easy. Mostly, it's just about listening to other people talk and then chiming in with your life experiences or taking notes from what they're talking about and forming questions to ask them. This is the key to a good conversation. It's the key to a first great date which could lead to a great second date and so on and so forth.

Being a good conversationalist entails being a good listener. You can also ask him about his job, his family and what sports he's into. Getting him talking about his life will attract more conversation and that's the Law of Attraction in action. Soon enough, the date will be over and you'll both want to keep talking.

One way to be a good conversationalist is to always have a subject on hand when the conversation turns dull. Don't be afraid to change the subject, either. Just do it. Your date will be relieved, especially if he's a little shy or a little smitten on you. (This is a good way to tell if he really, really likes you—he doesn't talk much and sometime stammers.

Real cute and points in your favor!) So, in order to draw on a variety of subjects, just study up on pop culture. Read a biography of your favorite author or actress or artist or whatever. This will come in handy when the conversation slows, believe me. Always educate yourself, even if you graduated years ago. Keep the wheels in your mind spinning and lube them by knowledge. Knowledge is power, even if that is a dorky thing to say. And, hey, if it wins points with some dreamboat, all the better.

Desperate, but not serious.

This is the title to a great song from the 80s by Adam Ant, and it is loosely related to the topic of this chapter—desperation.

Desperation in anyone is a big turnoff. Unfortunately, for many of us, we don't know when we're being desperate. However, it's good to be aware of this so you can avoid it, if at all possible. Seriously, don't be desperate.

When you come off as needy—desperate—it makes people uncomfortable, particularly guys. When you come off as *having* to be wanted, it makes people cringe. It's like you're trying too hard and when a person does this, it can be a little suspect. Even if this person has good intentions, it makes other people turn away.

Most men, generally speaking, like strong women. They like women who know what they want and who don't "need" a man. This makes them feel like they're joining in on your good time. However, when you overtly want someone, it comes off as partially suspect, partially disingenuous. And you come off as needy. And who wants to do that?

The good thing about this is all you have to do is begin to monitor yourself a bit. I'm not saying to change your whole demeanor, but it is necessary to know when to pull back so when you get the opportunity to meet a good guy, you don't come across as desperate. Hey, you're just there for a good time, too, right? You're just there at the club to party or at the bookstore to find a good book to read. That's the attitude you need in order for men to really want to get to know you. This may lead them to believe you have an allure of mystery and mystery in any woman is a huge aphrodisiac to any man.

It's like this, "She's interesting, but not quite interested in me. Huh? What can I do about that?" By acting like this and not giving off any vibe of desperation, this gets the wheels turning in his mind and, soon enough, he's going to want to know you better.

The gist is: If you act like your life depends on some guy or some date, you'll never find a decent man. To not act desperate, all you have to do is a few simple things…

You have to:
- Leave them wanting more.
- Not try too hard.
- Dress appropriately but never slutty.
- Don't ever have sex on the first date. (It will only be the exceptionally rare occasion that you find a man who will appreciate your lack of inhibition, believe me.)

And this is so easy to do. However, I have seen the complete opposite a million times. A girl will like a guy and, if he shows a morsel of interest, she will smother him. On the other hand, I've seen it work in the opposite way. If a girl catches a guy's eye and gives him a little attention, then turns away, he goes nuts with desire for her. She's something he can't have. Therefore, he *has* to have her. This builds desire, want and need. This is what you're after. You want to be wanted and this is how you do it. But you can't do it if you act the least bit desperate.

Keep in mind, you can never bulldog your way into anyone's life. If you start to push in, they will pull back. It's just a natural human response. *Why is she so interested in me? Is there something wrong with her?* There's probably nothing wrong, it just makes guys, and people in general, uneasy when anyone desperately wants into their lives. Sure, it may be coming from a place of "eager to please" but being too eager equals looking desperate. But just going with the flow and not being desperate means you don't have to take much of anything too seriously. When you take desperation out of the scenario, see how fun your life will become.

Again, the Law of Attraction is like attracts like. So, if you come off as being desperate, you might get a guy who's as desperate as you. Not so much fun. Keep in mind that when you're desperate, you're worried about the how. So, get off the "how" and get to the fun stuff.

So, I say, just relax and don't be desperate, and certainly not serious. And it might not be a bad idea to have that song running through your head whenever you go out. Hey, it's a reminder to take life—and men—a little less seriously. That way, you can begin to attract men into your life who are interested in you and not turned off by any sort of desperation.

It's up to him to do the asking.

It's up to him to do the asking. So, you've done everything you need to do. You've figured out what you want and you've released and then waited for inspiration. Then you had an idea of how to meet someone. And then you did it. Then you found the man you want. Now what? What do you do now? How do you take it to the next level, per se?

Listen very carefully: *You let him do the asking. You don't do anything.*

"What? I've done all this work and now I have to wait on this jerk to ask me out?" Yes you do and I'll tell you why. You never ask a man out on a date and you never ask for his number. Well, you can, but it puts you in a very different position than you would've been had you allowed him to do this. I, personally, don't think there's anything wrong with asking a man out on a date. However, I do advise taking it case by case. If you find that maybe he is just too shy or whatever, then it's okay. However, I also believe it's quite possible to put your want out there, as in, "I want Joe to ask me out," and have it happen. Anything is possible. Why not try it?

However, I also believe that it's best to just wait and let him do the work. Why? Because if he doesn't make the effort, that means he's not that interested. I don't care how cute he is or what excuse he has for not doing it—like because he's busy or inhibited or whatever—he has to be the one to ask for the date. He has to "man-up", to use a popular phrase. So, wait for him to do the work. If he lets this opportunity pass him by, then that's his loss. And you move on to someone who will take the effort to ask you out.

This can be a very hard pill to swallow. But it really doesn't work any other way. Believe me, if a man really wants you, he won't let you pass him by. And if he doesn't? Then he doesn't. Nothing you can do about it, either. However, if you are implementing the Law of Attraction, you *will* find someone who will want to do the asking. All you have to do is put your want out there and allow it to come to you. Soon enough, it will. Just be patient.

So, let him do the asking. If you jump the gun and ask him out, it will set the tone for your entire relationship—*she's in control and I don't have a say-so on anything.* And while you will basically be in control anyway, he doesn't have to know that.

Artificial deadlines.

Get rid of any artificial deadlines you may have. By this I mean, we all place deadlines on ourselves to get things done. In essence, we say to ourselves, "I have to do this or that by a certain age." A lot of women want to be married and/or have babies by a certain date. Or they want to be successful. Or they want to have X-amount of money in the bank or drive a certain car or wear a certain designer shoe. Or whatever. This means they are placing artificial deadlines on themselves. And therefore, by doing this, they are blocking a lot of other good stuff from entering their lives.

In today's world, women can be married and not have kids, and vice versa. So, just because one doesn't follow the other, doesn't mean we shouldn't do what we want to do. What you have to do is let go of exactly what you want so it can enter in your life in other ways.

With the Law of Attraction, you will pretty much get what you want; however, it may not be in the form you think it will. It might not happen exactly how you want, and that's okay, as long as you get it. By letting go of artificial deadlines, you will put yourself in the forefront of receiving what you want. You will open yourself up to new options that you hadn't thought of before. It doesn't have to be by this date or that date, as long as you get it, right? Right. Remember when I said to let go of the "how"? This is one way to let go of the how and that's by letting go of something you want so it can manifest.

Putting a deadline on anything is a sure-fire way to insure it won't happen. Believe me, I know. Once you do that, you're basically saying: "I will have this by this date." Well, it doesn't really work like that. Other stuff might have to happen to get you to that point. And if you have a deadline, other stuff will have trouble happening because it isn't happening in the exact way you want. And this means that by doing this to yourself, you are almost insuring that you will never get what you want. when you don't get things in the way you expect, you may not appreciate it and you will block other things from happening. And all because you put a deadline on your happiness.

Can't do that. Shouldn't do that. Stop doing that. Happiness will come once you give it the chance. Deadlines are fear based and we all know that anything that is fear based sucks the joy out of life. Which is not what we're after here.

Don't be anybody's victim.

Don't be anybody's victim. In life, things happen and sometimes we end up being victims of someone else's betrayal. This can hurt an awful lot, believe me. However, once it's over, let it be over. Don't keep being someone's victim by holding onto what happened whenever it happened.

You can't control everything. Sometimes, bad things just happen. It happens to the best of us, too. That's life. We can't control everything that goes on in our lives and, most importantly, we can't control anyone else, either. What other people do is up to other people. If our feelings get in the way and get hurt, then that's what sometimes happens.

And yet, knowing this, many of us hold onto our past hurts. We wear them like a badge of honor—"They won't get the best of me!" Well, guess what? They *are* getting the best of you and they're getting it because you're allowing yourself to still be their victim.

So, are you happy being someone's victim? No, you can't be. No one is happy being someone's victim. Being a victim entitles you to a lifetime of pure, unadulterated misery. That's all you get out of it. While they're tra-la-laing it on down the line, you're still simmering about what has happened. Do you think they care? Do you think they're hurting? More than likely not. Harsh reality, huh?

Life is all about perception. What can be a bump in the road to others, can torment some. But if you change your perception on the situation, you can begin to let go. Instead of beating yourself up over something that happened, you can say, "I was young, naïve, and, therefore, was ripe for someone to take advantage of me." You can get over it, just by changing how you perceive it.

But sometimes it just happens to us. A time or two it's happened to me. But one day, I woke up and realized the most important aspect to all of this and that was: *It has nothing to do with me.* What other people do to us has nothing to do with us. It's true. When I look back on my life, I realize that I have taken too much responsibility for things that have been done to me. I've always felt a little too responsible for other people's feelings. But one day, I realized I wasn't responsible for other people's feelings, just like they're not responsible for mine. We all have to take personal responsibility for ourselves, feelings and all.

So, basically what I began to say to myself was, "That had nothing to do with me." And when you look at the situation, no matter how cringe-worthy is, can't you see that, too? What did it have to do with you? Did you incite it? Did you instigate it? What was your part?

If you are on the receiving end of this, you probably had very little to do with it. So, let go of the victim mode. Being in victim mode will not serve you in any way, shape or form.

Like I said, it's all about changing perspective and if you can do that and stop being other's victim, you will start allowing the Law of Attraction to work. And then you can be happy! Once you put a stop to it, then you can really start on the path to finding a good man. You can date the man you most desire and getting out of the victim mode is a step in the right direction.

Say it with me: "That has nothing to do with me."

What is in the past is in the past. Once you actually get this and get past all this "bad stuff", good stuff will come into your life. Keep in mind that once something "bad" happens, we get into a place of fear—that more bad stuff will happen. And so it does. We attract it. Yes, we do. We attract this over and over, especially if we are in victim mode. It might feel uncomfortable to acknowledge this, but it's the truth. Sure, sometimes it's safe and kinda fun to wallow in our victim mindset and go back over past events. Sure, sometimes, it might feel good for a minute. But allowing that one minute to turn into days and years of built-up resentment can only lead to one thing: Supreme unhappiness.

So, do yourself a favor now—wipe your slate clean. Start over. Start fresh. All the things in the past don't matter now, they just don't matter. So, let go of them. Whenever they arise in your mind, say to yourself, "That doesn't matter anymore." Soon enough, it won't and that's because you're letting go, you're releasing and, in the process, you are reclaiming your power!

Wipe everything off your slate. Wipe away friends who've done you wrong, boyfriends who left without a good reason, men who've used you or not called back and wipe it clean for good. Another good thing to eliminate are your past wants, things you didn't get to do but might be niggling at you still. Get rid of them. Come back to them in time and see if they still fit in your life.

And, again, say to yourself, "This stuff doesn't matter anymore" and also, "This has nothing to do with me." And you know what? It really doesn't.

A nice bottle of perfume.

Most of us have this one bottle of perfume that we're saving for something, which means we're waiting on a special occasion to use it. Or maybe we're waiting until we've used all the other bottles of perfume that clutter our medicine cabinets before we start on this one. Maybe we're not using it because it was so expensive. Whatever the reason is irrelevant, but if we want to get into a place where we are accepting more great things into our lives, one way is to start using that bottle of perfume we've been saving.

Of course, I am speaking symbolically. "Saving" anything like a bottle of perfume is representative of how one is viewing their life. Are you also saving yourself, as well? Are you saving yourself for the perfect man, accompanied by the perfect situation?

It might not even be a bottle of perfume you're saving. It could be a bottle of wine or a nice dress or a pair of shoes. But we all have something we're saving for that time in our lives when we really want to celebrate. I say, why wait until later? Celebrate today! Get that stuff out and use it! If you run out, you can always get more, right?

By celebrating today, you are using the Law of Attraction to bring more good things into our lives. But by holding off on using something we already have, by "saving" it, it's kind of like we don't even have it. When we do this, we are, in effect, waiting to enjoy our lives. Seriously, people who do this are waiting to enjoy their lives. And guess what?

They're going to be waiting for a long time. Until you make the conscious decision to enjoy life, starting today, you'll never have an occasion to celebrate. *Today is good enough!* You can enjoy today for no other reason than that you've lived another day. That's a good a reason as anyone needs, isn't it?

And you might not know it, but perfume goes bad after a while, so it's pointless to save it. (Wine, too, can go bad after a while—especially Sauvignon Blanc!) Take that approach with everything in your life and you will soon see that saving a bottle of perfume or whatever is just coming from a place of lack.

And, perhaps, stop saving yourself. Begin to put yourself out there for better dating experiences. Remember, time is a'wastin'!

If you don't have a nice bottle of perfume, buy one and use it everyday. Whenever you spray it on, take a deep breath and smile. Luxuriate in it. It's *yours*. It smells nice, right? It makes you feel nice, right? That's the mind frame we're looking for.

You have to get over your heartbreak.

You have to get over your heartbreak. When we think of heartbreak, we usually think of it in the traditional sense of a man and a woman, as in a man breaks a woman's heart, or vice versa. But that's not the only heartbreak a person can experience. Other people in our lives can break our hearts, too.

Years ago, I personally experienced a big heartbreak where an authority figure betrayed me. I didn't have a lot invested in this relationship emotionally, but once it happened, I felt like I'd been hit by a ton of bricks. *I had trusted this person.* Coincidentally, this led to the demise of a dream job I'd had for years and I experienced major heartbreak. All this was because he decided he didn't like me well enough to want me in that position. I had been completely oblivious to his attitude towards me.

However, I never reconciled the loss of my dream, nor did I recognize that I'd actually gone through heartbreak. It took me years to realize this, years of self-doubt and years of wondering why I felt so bad about myself because this one thing didn't happen for me. It was only when I dealt with my feelings regarding this matter that it began to bother me less. Soon enough, it was done and all that was left was a little bitterness which, in time, also dissolved.

When we experience heartbreak in this way, we don't feel okay. With a guy, we can rebound. Not so with an authority figure like this. It's almost impossible. And, so, we begin to feel that we have to compensate for this loss. We might have something we think we can do or obtain that will make us feel better, that will make us feel okay. *Once we do this, everything will be fine and get back in order.* Until we get it, we will not feel okay. This could be a dream to move somewhere or get a better job, boyfriend, or car. It could be anything, but it is the one thing that we think will make us feel okay once again.

Unfortunately, this feeling is exactly what we're getting back, the feeling of lack, the feeling we'll never get what we want—the feeling that we're not okay. Then it becomes a *need* to make us okay and need is born out of fear. And that just exacerbates the situation. Soon enough, we're depressed, hurting and angry. *How did my life turn out like this? All because of this guy or that girl? Because of my mother?* No, because something happened that made us believe we're not okay and that set all this other stuff into action.

Heartbreak of this kind can also taint any future relationship you might have with a man. Or it could lead to repeating the same mistakes over and over.

So, what can we do? Understand that not only can authority figures hurt us, but others who supposedly care for us can too. Mothers can be big heartbreakers. And fathers. And just about anyone a young person is supposed to trust. We have to realize that in the real world—and I've said this before—stuff happens. I'm not saying that we need to defend the hurtful, hateful things that are done to us, but we do need to recognize that we have been hurt. And being hurt sucks. But for many of us, we have to keep a stiff upper lip. We can't show others the damage they've done. And, therefore, we can't reconcile our feelings.

I'm not saying, of course, to start pointing fingers or go on some talk show or whatever. I'm just saying that when we push our feeling down and don't experience them as they happen, we begin to collect emotional baggage, or, as I like to call it, emotional garbage. We take this emotional garbage around everywhere we go and we carry it into any new relationship we have. Soon enough, the garbage begins to stink and has to be dealt with. The problem is, many people don't deal with it and it leads to the demise of important relationships. It also leads to a pretty crappy life full of negativity and frustration.

When we've been heartbroken, we expect disappointment and so we get it, time and time again. Reconcile it. Sit down and feel your heartbreak. Cry if necessary. Let out those feelings that you've been carrying around. Get rid of your emotional garbage.

We're sensitive souls; otherwise no one would be able to break our hearts. But this doesn't mean we can't get over the hurt when something "bad" happens. And how do we get over it? We forgive.

Granted, forgiveness is tough. The wounds we feel might be too open for immediate forgiveness. But this isn't a reason to allow them to fester. Give it some time. Feel your feelings and allow them to dissolve on their own. Soon, enough, you are ready to forgive.

But how do we forgive? Practice. Once you're ready, just start forgiving the person who has hurt you. "I forgive _____ for _____." It might feel a little fake at first, like you're lying to yourself. But I like to think about it like I'm moving past the hurt each time I say this to myself. And, soon enough, I am. Soon enough, I can forgive and then forget.

You have to realize that we cannot forget if we do not first forgive. It is the biggest gift you will ever give yourself and that's because, once it's done, you can set that baggage of heartbreak down and walk away from it. You don't have to keep bringing it up over and over in your mind and trying to find out "why" you feel so bad. You just have to let go. Release the pain and move forward. The good news is that this also works for guys who've hurt you, too. Releasing these men out of your life by forgiving them not only feels good, but it opens you up to better guys.

All of this can be a great learning experience, too. You can learn many things about yourself from heartbreak, such as your boundaries and your sensibilities. What you may have put up with in your past doesn't mean you have to put up with it in your future. It's all about learning about what not to do so you can do better.

Once you begin to do this, you will allow many good new things into your life. Hanging onto heartbreak of any kind is a recipe for an unhappy life and it will block the magic of the Law of Attraction from happening.

You never win by losing.

By putting yourself down, by denying your wants, by delving into negativity or by allowing others to stand in your way of happiness, you never win. You always lose. And you can never win by losing. And if you never even participate? You lose there, too.

Whenever you find yourself looking for fault in yourself, you are putting yourself down. Sometimes we do this because we want to fit in. I can remember a friend of mine who went through a great transformation. She lost weight, she cut her hair in a stylish manner and she started looking for a better job. However, once she did this, she noticed that everyone around her began to get a little uncomfortable because she was making big—but good—changes in her life. So, she withdrew from what she wanted—life transformation—and began to put herself down just to keep fitting in with her friends. The problem was, she'd outgrown these people but was afraid to move on. She lost out on a many good life experiences because she was afraid to do what was best for herself. Shame, really. What's worse is that in order to fit in again, she reverted back to her old "losing" self and she gained her weight back and stopped her life transformation.

Along with this, we also get into the habit of denying what we really want out of life. Of course, getting to the point of knowing what we want can be challenging. But it doesn't have to be. The problem we have with this is that we feel like we don't deserve what we want, so we stay in a constant state of denial. This doesn't bode well for anyone and can creep into other areas of your life, making you feel terrible. And you lose.

Additionally, whenever we delve into negativity, we're again losing in life. This is because negativity can be soul crushing, as I said earlier. No good can come from negativity but for some reason, we think that negativity protects us and somehow by looking at things in this way, we can always come out on top. This won't ever happen because you've entrusted negativity with your happiness and that means, even if you get what you want, you won't ever be happy with it. So, you lose.

Many times in life, we hesitate to do exactly what we want to do because we're afraid it might "hurt" someone else. This could be through embarrassment or what they might perceive as a betrayal. Or it could be that they might see our "moving on up" as leaving them behind. Whatever the reason, we sometimes forget what we want just because we don't want others to feel uncomfortable at what we're doing. This is also a losing situation.

This all means that if you make yourself out to be a non-participant, you will never win—ever! But for some reason, we think if we take ourselves out of the competition—by allowing negativity to take over, etc.— then we will win. This is nothing more than playing it safe and to always play it safe means that's all you'll ever do.

You can't please everyone. In fact, I'd venture to say, you can rarely please anyone, except yourself. But by thinking you can hold yourself back and always play it safe and somehow still win at life, you're doing yourself a great disservice. Life doesn't have to be a competition, but if you never take that first step, you will always end up losing. And how can you ever be wanted if you never put yourself in the race? You can't.

So never think you can win by losing. You're just fooling yourself and setting yourself up for a great disappointment.

The point of this chapter is this: Whenever you hold yourself back from doing anything you truly want, because of whatever reason, you are not playing at life. And if you can never play, you can never win.

Background noise.

Have you ever been at a busy airport or grocery store? Of course you have. Regardless of how noisy or hectic these places are, you eventually become oblivious to the chaos that's going on, right? And that's because you're focused on what you have to do—hop on a plane or pick up some laundry detergent and bread. Everything that is in the background—all the noise and chaos—fades into the background, where it should be. You don't notice it because, really, it's got nothing to do with you.

Buzzzzz... hear it? That's background noise. In and of itself, it's not so bad. What's bad is when background noise suddenly comes to the forefront of your mind and takes over. When this happens, all you will hear is noise and you'll not only be a little confused about what you want out of life, but confused about everything. Who cares about finding a man? I've got all this other stuff going on in my head! When this happens, you're paying too much attention to the background noise.

So what is background noise? Background noise, among other things, is everyone else's opinion about what you should do with your life. It's everyone else's fears. It's their problems, their wants. It's really nothing to do with you. But, for some reason, we tend to start tuning into the background noise and, once we do that, it gets louder and louder, so our focus gets skewed. In essence, we get so focused on what others expect of us, we forget about our original intentions. *What am I really doing? Shouldn't I be focused on other things instead of just myself and my wants? Maybe I should put off going out on dates and finding a decent man for a while. Yeah, I don't need that right now anyway.*

Background noise is anything—especially unimportant stuff—that distracts you from what you really want. And, many times, it can come in the form of self doubt. When background noise causes self doubt, it buzzes around inside your head until it almost drives you insane. "I don't know if I can do this, should do this, will do this... I just don't know!" Soon enough, you're so afraid of making a mistake you end up doing nothing!

When this happens, it means we're tuning into the background noise. Once we do this, chaos will ensue in our lives. I've wanted to do many things so badly in my life and was gung-ho to do so. But once I started talking about it to others, I realized it might not be such a good idea. Doubt set in, along with fear. *What if I can't do this?* I was tuning into background noise.

You might still be thinking, "But if I don't try to help others with their problems, I'm being selfish." No. Like I said, it's not our jobs to fix anyone else. By not trying to solve all problems, it forces others to take responsibility for themselves, which is what they should have been doing in the first place. Sure, we all like to vent every once in a while, but if you're listening to a new problem everyday, it will take over your life.

This is not to say to not help anyone else ever again. You really can help other people; you just can't do it at the expense of yourself or your sanity or let their problems become your problems. And if you're so focused on everyone else, you're not focused on yourself enough and when this or that happens, there's no way you can open yourself up to better dating experiences.

People who succeed stay focused on what they want. Women who stay focused on what they want—getting a good boyfriend or marriage or kids or career—always get what they want. They don't let others dissuade them from it, either. They know everyone won't approve, but they have to do whatever it is they want to do, which will make them happy. But many of us tune into what others are saying and begin to doubt ourselves. We don't want to hurt anyone's feelings, after all and going after our dreams just might make others shake in their boots a little.

Sounds ridiculous, doesn't it? But it's so true. People resent other people who go after what they want and they do this because they're afraid to get what *they* want out of life. You have to be prepared that people in your life might fall by the wayside. Good news—you get to trim the fat without ever doing anything! And this means you can welcome better, more positive people into your life. I have lost several good friends over this, over *succeeding*. Well, obviously they weren't very good friends to begin with or they would have been happy for me. You might find that this happens to you, too. It's sad but true.

At first, when you start getting what you want out of life, people might start acting strangely towards you and they might start withdrawing. They're jealous! Don't feel bad, though. This is their problem. But they won't take off until they've instilled some self-doubt in you. In effect, they will say, "Are you sure you want to do this? Are you sure you want to go through with it?" Soon enough, you're not sure and a little panicked! This is some major change, it might be best to sit back and let it ride.

By doing this, you are doing yourself a major disservice. Once you start listening to others in this way, you will stop thinking for yourself and, therefore, doing for yourself. Your life will be about everyone else and nothing about what you want, which is to find a good man.

You have to keep in mind that it is up to others to get what they want out of life, not you. You can inspire them, but they have to call their own intentions to the forefront. You can't fix anyone else, just as you can't make people get what they want out of life. You're not a genie in a bottle, after all. However, if you begin to listen to them by turning up that background noise, you're letting other people take over your life. When they do this, they're basically bullying you. You have to stand up to them and tell them to back off.

When you start hearing that background noise get louder, do yourself a favor and turn it down. This isn't about them, it's about you.

You gotta have faith.

You gotta have faith. And you do. When approaching any new situation, especially concerning matters of dating, we all get a little nervous, mostly because we worry that it might not work out. The problem with change is this: When you resist it, you *do* change, but usually not in the way you would like. Usually you get more nervous, agitated and angry. Some of us change into cowards.

However, if you have faith that everything is going to turn out okay, then you will be able to handle any bad situation. You might not like it, but you *will* be able to handle it. Say you might go on a bad few dates at first, but if you have faith one will turn out good, it will.

One way many of us show our lack of faith is by trying to control everything and one way we do that is by not stating our desires, while secretly really wanting them. We think that by "believing" it won't happen, it will. For some reason, we feel like we can't get what we want and we have to "trick" the universe into believing in us enough to go ahead and give it to us without ever actually wanting it. This is a supreme lack of belief in ourselves and a lack of faith. But we keep thinking: *It'll just happen! Surprise me!*

The big surprise is when it never happens. *But I wanted it so bad.* But you never acknowledged you did! Do you get what I'm saying?

It sounds convoluted, but many of us think that by actually not believing what we want will happen, it *will* happen. This is just another example of how we try to control things. But the opposite is true. By really believing we can receive what we want, we can have it. The question then becomes: Why do we do this to ourselves? And the answer is easy: We think that by stating our desires, we will somehow jinx it. So, we keep them under wraps, hoping that we will somehow get what want. When that happens, we won't have a chance of getting what we want. By doing this, we cheat ourselves out of it. Why do we do this? I believe this is something that many of us are taught or scared into thinking.

It's almost like not believing in something is a security blanket protecting us from disappointment. By not believing, we are shielding ourselves from all kinds of "bad" feelings—frustration, dissatisfaction, you name it. And, again, quite the opposite is true because then we have the double whammy of not getting what we want and the disappointment that follows. All because we were afraid to believe we could ever get what we wanted. And yet we persist with this tortuous way of looking at things—by not believing in it, we think it stands a much better chance of happening.

It's like we say to ourselves, "Oh, I don't have to worry about that ever happening because it never will." Maybe we think it will happen that much more quickly. Wrong! Maybe we think this is the way we give up control, so it can happen. Wrong again! We think that by pretending to not want something, we will get it. Again, the opposite is true. This strange belief is what has kept many people from getting to the next level of life, from experiencing true success. This is what keeps many good women from finding good men.

Is it what's keeping you from getting what you want? Many of us do it on a subconscious level. I did it, too, without even realizing it until one day, I caught myself.

Once I realized what I was doing, I was able to correct the situation.

This book is about getting what you want. But you have to be able to state what you want and then believe it will happen. This means letting go of control. This means having faith.

Part of having faith is giving up control. This is hard for most people but you have to trust. Having faith means you do give up control. This isn't bad. It simply means you would no longer have a fear of losing control, which can lead to panic, because you have faith. Whenever you embark on anything new such as getting what you really and truly want out of life, you can feel a little squeamish. You have to have faith that you will be able to handle anything that's thrown at you. You have to have faith that everything will turn out okay.

And it usually does, doesn't it?

Ask yourself: *Can I handle it if it doesn't work out?* Of course you can! This is because you will know that even if this one thing doesn't work out, something else will. This is where faith kicks in.

So, do you have faith? One way to tell is to take notice of your life. Have you made room in your life for your perfect man? Are you ready for him to enter? Have you already met someone, but he's not quite right? Sure, he's perfect but... He's got kids. He has nose hair. His job sucks. He's too this or he's too that. No, no, no! Do you like him? If, yes, then go for it!

This is having faith!

Still, you might be thinking, "He's good, but just not that *good*. If I give in, I'll never get what I want." Again, this is where faith kicks in. You have to get to the point where you eventually have to give in. Remember we talked about resistance? Resistance is the opposite of giving in, releasing.

It's control—fear of losing control! By never allowing it to happen, it won't ever happen.

And, like I said, this is where faith kicks in. Once you have faith that everything will turn out okay, you can relax and go with the man you think might be the best. He might not turn out to be the best, but so what? That means you're on your way to the man who will be the best. But, without faith, neither of these guys will ever measure up.

So, you gotta have faith. So, get some.

Stand still. Look pretty.

My, don't you look pretty today?

Who me? Oh, this old thing? I bought it two years ago, on sale. My hair? I don't know what's going on with it today. It actually looks nice! Can you believe it? These shoes? Oh, they're scuffed up and tattered. They kinda do look cool, but I really need some new ones.

What the heck are you doing? You know what you're doing. You're getting complimented but your old friend, self-doubt, has risen to the occasion to take it away from you.

We've all done this. We don't want to take compliments because it puts us in a position of feeling uncomfortable. It might be that we know we look good, but we have to run ourselves down in case others don't look as good as we do. It might be that we really do think we look awful and can't believe anyone would say we look pretty.

Get over yourself. Seriously, get over yourself. And learn to take a compliment.

If you want to be wanted—and who doesn't?—you have to be willing to embrace yourself. But, for some of us, insecurity steps in and takes over to the point that if someone compliments anything about us—from our clothes to our cat—we can't take it. *They must be blind!* No, but you just might be.

The Law of Attraction works by us embracing everything in our lives, but one of the main things we don't embrace is ourselves. We look into the mirror and just see all of our flaws. I do this and I am quite sure you do, too. It's something most women do. We focus so much on what's wrong, we can't see anything that is right.

So, find one thing you like about yourself and start to really embrace it. It could be your eyes, your complexion, your legs—whatever, just embrace it. Even if you feel like you look awful on any given day, embrace your good feature. This is a good one: *I have beautiful eyes.* Or, my favorite: *I am a sexy bitch!* Say it to yourself, right now: *I am a sexy bitch!* See? Don't you feel better about yourself? You should!

What you're doing when you do this is basic thought replacement. Instead of looking into the mirror and tearing yourself down, you look into the mirror and tell yourself how good you look, even if it feels a little false at first. This builds self esteem. And you are showing yourself that you are accepting yourself when before you were basically shaming yourself.

Everyone has at least one good feature and you just need to accentuate your best one. Keep in mind that guys like different things and will find beauty in things most women overlook. For example, if you think your nose is too big, I can guarantee you that there are a lot of guys who will love it. The same goes with about every other feature you somehow dislike about yourself.

Going after what you want will take some effort. But it's not hard work. It should be work you enjoy doing. By embracing yourself and then by expanding on what you do like, you can begin to work on the things you don't like. If this means you have to lose weight or see a dermatologist or get a new wardrobe, then that's what it mean. Just do it. This is kind of like forming a habit, but once you get started, it's becomes just that—a habit. So, start today to totally accept and love yourself. Make it a habit you don't want to break!

Keep in mind that you have to have something that will pique a guy's attention. Unfortunately, men are attracted by looks. Always have and always will. This is the way they are genetically designed. So, is it any accident that women are so concerned with their looks? With looking pretty for men? No. If you don't stand out a little, he won't notice you. So, what do you do to attract men? You stand still and look pretty.

Don't worry about having movie star good looks because nowadays, a lot of movie stars don't have them either. All you have to do is dress nicely to show off your body without showing off too much and get into shape. Also, get a nice hairstyle and always have your nails done. Most of us do all this stuff, anyway, so it won't be a problem.

But most importantly, start loving yourself, and, if you can't love, at least start to like. This little step towards embracing yourself is all you need to get started on a lifetime of self acceptance. Once you do that, you might just find that others start to accept you too, and want you in their lives. And, again, like attracts like, so if you like yourself, others will like you too.

Death to marriage? Or, rather, death to discussing marriage.

Marriage has become a dirty word. Everyone wants to keep their options open. No one wants that lifelong commitment. Well, we do, but we don't want anyone to *think* we do. However, marriage isn't what it used to be. Today, it seems to be more of an albatross, something you avoid as long as possible and when you do get in, you hop out of once it gets tough. Well, that might not be the way women see it, but a lot of men see it this way.

And yet, most women still want it. Most women want a beautiful wedding and kids and a white picket fence. So what? It's a good want. But men these days aren't so sure. They want to play around, go to ballgames and be perpetual bastards. I mean, *bachelors*.

So, it's a fine line we walk, isn't it? You find the perfect guy but—guess what?—he doesn't want to get married. Surprise! He doesn't want to grow up! Shocker! He just doesn't know what he wants but he does know what he doesn't want and, most times, that's marriage.

But still, you probably want to know whether or not the man of your choosing will ever take the plunge with you, right? This is a slippery slope. However, my advice is this: Never mention marriage too early on. At least not until there's some kind of solid relationship going. You never want a guy to think you're thinking on those terms. But why? Because if you begin to mention it, he might begin to get antsy and think you're boxing him in, poor guy. (Note sarcasm.) In effect, you have to beat 'em at their own game.

I am not saying you have to take my advice or whatever. I am not saying unless you know beyond a shadow of a doubt that he wants to get married, you can't get a guy to marry you by you first mentioning it. I'm just saying it's usually best if it's his idea. However, you can mention it to test the waters whenever you like. See how he reacts. If he gets jittery, then he might just be a runner. If he's open from the get-go, you might just have a winner. The key is to use discretion.

We all know that men tend to run from marriage. So, beat 'em at their own game. In fact, even if they do mention it, change the subject. This will get the wheels turning in their heads: *Does she like me or not? I said something about marriage and now she's acting a little aloof.*

Huh. How about that? Now he knows how you feel. Good on you. Too bad for him.

Don't talk about it; don't discuss it, just stay away from the subject, even if it's what you want. This is especially important in the first part of any relationship. But, like I said, once you know he's in love with you, you might casually mention it to test the water and see where his mind's at. However, I have seen many women jump the gun after they've dated a guy for a few months and start talking about marriage and kids. And, usually, the guy bails. This is why you have to use caution about the subject of marriage. Keep in mind that if it is what you want, you will have it but you do have to release. Remember how we talked about releasing? So, release it. Sure, state your desire, but then release. You *have* to release.

But what if he never mentions marriage? In these days and times, this is a real possibility and that's where the Law of Attraction kicks in. Once you find the guy you know will make you a good husband, simply state your want—just not to him: "I want to marry him." And then see if it manifests. If he's thinking the same thing—remember like attracts like—he's going to pop the question. And if he's not? He probably won't. And then you need to move on to someone who will want to get married.

You will know if he's interested. And don't lie to yourself about it, either. If he's not interested, you move on to the next guy. And if he's not interested? You keep moving on until you eventually find someone who wants what you want—marriage. *Like attracts like.*

If marriage is your ultimate desire, you will have it. It might not be with certain commitment-phobic guys, but it will be with someone who wants it as much as you do. So, hold out for the genuine article. It won't be long before you have it if you use the Law of Attraction to bring it into you life.

Never wait for a man.

Never wait for a man. Never wait by the phone. Never wait on him at a restaurant, unless he calls and says he's running late. Never wait for man, period. And why? Because you don't have to. If he can't call you, if he can't show up on time, forget him. And another thing, if he has to ask you out via a text message, he isn't worth it. I mean, you're at least worth a phone call, right? Right.

We've all been through it. He said he'd call… He didn't. So what? Screw him! Say it with me, ladies: Screw him! Now go out and find yourself a guy who will call when he says he will.

I absolutely hate it when guys play this stupid phone/waiting game. I say, beat him at his own game and don't be waiting by the phone. When he sees that life goes on with or without him, he'll straighten up. Or, perhaps, he might realize he's just missed his chance with you.

Make it a simple rule: Don't wait. Dating is so complicated these days. You can't show you're interested, you can't call. Forget that. Make a vow to simplify your dating life. And start by not playing the "waiting by the phone" game. Life is too short for that.

Of course, there may be extenuating circumstances like he might have been involved in an accident or attacked by wolves or the dog ate his homework or whatever. If this happens, of course, give him another chance. The key is to use your brain with any circumstance but never allow yourself to be stood up. Use your best judgment but if too many calamities happen to him, he might just be lying. And that means he's not worth a second of your time.

Say thank you.

Every day, make a point to be appreciative of how far you've come. Everyday say thanks. It used to be, people would say a blessing before each meal. Now, we just take it for granted and dive right in. It shouldn't be like this.

One way to really activate the Law of Attraction is by showing gratitude. Sometimes it's hard to find gratitude, I know, but try to do this. Once you show how much you appreciate what you have, you will stand a better chance of getting more of what you want.

After you say thank you, why not spread your blessing? Why not give thanks and show gratitude by helping out others who are less fortunate? Why not donate some time or money or some old junk that you're not using anymore? Why not help someone? The more you give, the more you will get. This works wonders by showing that you have faith in knowing you will be okay, so it becomes okay to give.

So, say thank you. Appreciate what you have. Give to others that are less fortunate. Spread the wealth, spread the joy. And watch how your life changes before your very eyes.

The Law of Attraction isn't that hard to figure out. Dating, on the other hand, can be quite complicated. Figure out exactly what you don't want and from that you will find your want, your true desire. Once you figure it out, say you want it. Feel the freedom of stating what you want out of life. And then release it. You can start enjoying your life. But then don't be surprised when your desire happens, when it's manifested. Life will become that much sweeter.

One reason we can't say what we want is out of fear that it might not happen. But fear is nothing more than a guidepost showing us the way to what we truly desire. Sure, it might not happen. But what if it does?

So, say it, "What if I can really get everything I want out of life? What if I can get the man I most desire, who will desire me and I can have the life I deserve?"

Now, close your eyes and savor the possibilities. That's exciting, isn't it? Don't you feel the passion? Once you feel it, you will have it. So, enjoy it.